A SKILLET FULL

OF TRADITIONAL SOUTHERN
MEMORIES & RECIPES

Compiled by the Historic Preservation Society
of South Pittsburg, Tennessee
Hometown of Lodge Cast Iron

Compiled by the
South Pittsburg Historic Preservation Society, Inc.
Edited by Jeanne Scholze, Carolyn Millhiser & Barbara Clepper
Cover Illustrations and Design by Lodge Cast Iron
Cover Photo by Doug Barnette

Lodge Manufacturing Company
204 East 5th Street
South Pittsburg, TN 37380
www.lodgemfg.com
(423) 837-7181

Second Edition 2014
First Edition 2003

ISBN# 0-9677985-4-X

Printed in the United States of America

ACKNOWLEDGMENTS

Lodge Manufacturing gratefully acknowledges the members of our community who generously shared their favorite Lodge Cast Iron recipes with the world. We are also indebted to the members of the South Pittsburg Historic Preservation Society for accepting the daunting task of writing this book. As they accumulated recipes from the community, they gathered our cultural history.

Lodge is particularly grateful to the cookbook committee, Barbara Gonce Clepper, Carolyn Kellermann Millhiser, and Jeanne Mynatt Scholze, for contributing countless hours gathering, organizing, and testing recipes. We are also grateful to their husbands who were great sports through taste testing hundreds of recipes - both successes and failures.

Carolyn, a great-granddaughter of Joseph Lodge and daughter of the third president of Lodge, recently restored the home that Joseph built and lived in throughout his life. Barbara was raised on the Joseph Lodge farm and developed a love of cast iron cookware early in life. Jeanne is employed by Lodge as Marketing Director and loves to cook in cast iron.

To demonstrate our appreciation, a portion of the proceeds of this book will be donated to the South Pittsburg Historic Preservation Society to help as they preserve the historic buildings of our hometown.

SOUTH PITTSBURG, TENNESSEE THE HOMETOWN OF LODGE

In 1873 James Bowron, a noted iron master from Stockton in Trent, England, purchased 3000 acres of land rich in coal and iron for the "Old English Company", a syndicate of Englishmen interested in developing the American iron industry. The acreage was located in the scenic Sequatchie Valley of Tennessee just 30 miles west of Chattanooga, and framed by the Tennessee River on one side and the Cumberland Plateau on the other. The town that developed was named South Pittsburg, no doubt a reflection of the belief that the city would become the "Pittsburg of the South". Blast furnaces were put into operation in the northern part of the town and four very fine houses were built for officers of the Old English Company.

F. P. Clute, a civil engineer, surveyed and platted the physical structure of the town. Included in the plat were residential and commercial lots, where in 1877, Joseph Lodge built his home and later, a foundry. The streets were numerically numbered from north to south, and the wide avenues were given the names of trees. Shade trees were planted along the streets and avenues. Mr. Clute's map, filed in 1887, is still in use today. Later, in 1930, the streets, designed with curbs and gutters, were paved with concrete. Sidewalks were also laid. At the time, concrete streets were most remarkable.

With the death of Mr. Bowron and three colleagues, there was a lack of finances and the land including the City of South Pittsburg was sold. The South Pittsburg City Company in 1886 purchased 4,000 acres including all the land formerly held by the Old English Company. The City Company listed among its assets two hotels, one bank, four 13 room residences, one brick storehouse, eighty-four tenement houses, a water reservoir with four miles of water pipe, a coal mine, a school building, and a post office building.

In 1990, much of the South Pittsburg residential area was placed on the National Register of Historic Places. It qualified for inclusion in the National Register because of its development following a preconceived town plan.

The approved district of more than 46 acres comprises the historic core of the town and is distinguished by examples of late 19th and 20th century housing styles, from Italianate to Colonial Revival. Renewed community interest in preserving sites rich in the history of the city has been the impetus for the formation of the South Pittsburg Historic Preservation Society.

Today, South Pittsburg is easily accessed by Interstate 24, which is very handy for folks visiting during the National Cornbread Festival that is held annually on the last weekend of April.

THE NATIONAL CORNBREAD FESTIVAL
South Pittsburg, Tennessee

Each year on the last weekend in April, tens of thousands of visitors converge on the tiny Tennessee town of South Pittsburg (population 3000) for the National Cornbread Festival, and pay homage to the Southern cornmeal staple. Festivities include a street dance, celebrity entertainment, crafts, and of course a cornbread championship cook-off.

From more than 1000 entries, a panel of judges narrow the field to 10 finalists, each of whom participate in a cook-off at the festival for first, second, and third place honors. The culinary finalists create main dish cornbread recipes using Martha White® cornmeal and a Lodge cast iron skillet. From Tex-mex, to seafood, and every combination in between, they're all delicious.

If you are interested in joining us in South Pittsburg for the festival just visit the official festival site www.nationalcornbread.com.

FIRST NATIONAL BANK BUILDING 1887
SOUTH PITTSBURG, TENNESSEE

TABLE OF CONTENTS

LODGE IS GRATEFUL
To all who donated their family's favorite recipes,
and to the South Pittsburg Historic Preservation Society.

1896: A VERY GOOD YEAR

1896 was a very good year. The modern Olympic Games began in Athens, Greece. The Klondike Gold Rush began, which became one of the greatest gold rushes in history. Utah became a state and later proclaimed the cast iron Dutch oven to be the state's official cooking pot. Fanny Farmer published her first cookbook "The Boston Cooking School Cook Book", which made cooking history by including specific instructions and accurate measurements. It was the year that Alfred Ochs, publisher of the Chattanooga Times, purchased the failing New York Times and made it one of the world's great newspapers. William McKinley was elected president, whose simple food preferences of fried eggs, bacon and Johnnycakes cooked in cast iron became standard fare at the White House.

In a tiny town along the banks of the Tennessee River, Joseph Lodge, at age 48, began a cast iron cookware foundry. Twenty-one U.S. Presidents and more than 100 years later, that organization still flourishes. Just as Mr. Ochs did at the New York Times, Joseph Lodge put in place an enduring standard of quality. Few companies can boast that products they made over 100 years ago are still in use today. Even fewer can state that, not only are those products still in high demand, but, with proper care, they can last for another hundred years and another and another.

But not all cast iron cookware is created equal. Even heat dispersion is required for perfectly pan-fried chicken, crispy-crusted cornbread, and slow-simmering stews. Our privately held metal formula was developed just for cookware. The metal is carefully monitored with every pour, a standard not found in any other cast iron foundry. Precision molds made with exacting tolerances produce the correct wall thickness for each item. The marriage of our metal, our molds, and our finish produces cookware with legendary cooking performance demanded by your grandmother and other great American chefs.

Each piece of iron cookware is still created by pouring molten iron into individual sand molds, as it has been since the 17th century. However, four generations of family management have directed many changes in equipment and procedures. The great-grandsons of Joseph Lodge now direct an automated, state of the art, environmentally friendly foundry, with many third and fourth generation employees. Because of the family tradition of commitment to people, to quality and to reinvestment, Lodge is not only the sole domestic cast iron cookware foundry, it is also America's oldest family owned cookware manufacturer.

THE HEAT LOVING METAL

The heat-loving nature of the treasured Metal Ferrous (better known as iron) is the reason that iron cookware has endured for hundreds of years. Iron cookware has survived as a favorite of cooks, enduring the development every new metal. Iron is not only a great conductor of heat, but delivers the best and most uniform heat dispersion. As well, cast iron cookware cooks food evenly while resisting scorching and burning. Now that's a fabulous quality for a skillet to have, and why it's difficult to pan fry chicken in anything else.

Iron also retains heat longer than any other cookware. An attribute that resulted in cast iron kettles becoming the first slow-cookers. In the 18th century, tight fitting lids appeared on the kettles and they came to be called "Dutch ovens". Some say they were so named for Holland, the country that birthed the dry sand casting process still in use today. Others say the name came from the Dutch traders traveling the Early American Colonies peddling their wares. Whatever their name, they are a simmering stew's best friend, and nothing slow-cooks a roast better. Just as in Colonial times, today no self-respecting Southern bride sets up housekeeping without one.

Whether cast iron cookware is on the stove top or in the oven, the cooking result is often hailed as better than that of any cookware. The fact that it's almost indestructible and can last for generations only underscores its remarkable value. A single cast iron skillet and Dutch oven may have often been the only two pieces of cookware early American families possessed. Certainly a few more pieces would make cooking meals a little more convenient, but with these two essentials you can serve up one great meal after another. In a world of fancy, high priced cookware, cast iron can out-cook the most expensive, 21st century, high-tech kitchenware.

The first iron kettles and pots date back to the 7th and 8th centuries, but by 16th century Europe, the art of casting iron was widespread and cast iron cookware had become a valued commodity. Although the Colonists brought their cast iron pots with them to the New World, soon they were casting skillets and kettles of their own. Iron cookware was treasured so much that George Washington's mother even specified the recipient of her cast iron kitchenware in her will.

Then President Thomas Jefferson engaged Lewis and Clark to explore America's new territory, acquired with the Louisiana Purchase. The Corps of Discovery discarded many things to lighten the load, but never their cast iron pots. In fact, the only manufactured items returning with them were their guns and their iron pots. Little did they know that this would become the preamble to the settling of the American West.

And settle we did, but never without our cast iron cookware. To make the journey to lay claim to their parcel of Western America, each settling family packed their Conestoga wagon with only their most necessary and cherished possessions. Needless to say, that always included their iron pots and skillets. During the Great American Gold Rush, no matter how hurried a fellow left his home to travel to the American West to hunt for gold, he never left without his iron cookware. Every chuck wagon was built with special compartments for the iron Dutch ovens and skillets and "Cookie" was the most important person on every cattle drive. Cast iron fed the colonists as they settled the American East, and it fed the settlers, hopeful gold miners, and cowboys as they settled the American West.

From the cannons of the Revolutionary War, to the iron-shod horses that carried settlers westward, and the skillets, kettles and Dutch ovens that fed the adventurous explorers across the Rocky Mountains, cast iron has been an integral part of the forging of the American experience.

Now as the 21st century begins, great chefs and good home cooks still have good cast iron cookware on their list of essentials. And probably always will. In the world of cookware, cast iron is a Mercedes. It just doesn't have the price tag.

Paul Revere, a blacksmith and silversmith by profession, is credited with the flanged lid of the camp Dutch oven. The flanged lid and bottom legs allow for a fire source to be under the pot and on the lid, making it an actual baking oven at the hearth or campfire.

ALL ABOUT SEASONING...
AND IT'S NOT SALT AND PEPPER

It's likely that there are as many opinions on seasoning cast iron as there are cast iron cooks. Preferences on what oil, how much, how hot to make the oven, and for how long to bake the utensil are as varying as recipes for sweet tea and cornbread. One fact is quite unarguable, cast iron has to be seasoned before use, unless you're fortunate enough to have pried a skillet from your grandmother's stash, or recently purchased factory seasoned Lodge cast iron cookware.

SEASONING LODGE CAST IRON

If you have a new piece of Lodge cast iron cookware, it is seasoned, ready to use right from the start. Seasoning is the process of vegetable oil absorbing into the pores of the iron, turning the gray skillet black and slick.

Need to re-season? Here's how to do it:
- Wash the cast iron cookware with hot, soapy water and a stiff brush.
- Rinse and dry completely.
- Spread a thin coat of vegetable oil all over the entire surface of the pan, including handle and exterior surfaces.
- Line the lower oven rack with aluminum foil (to catch drippings), and preheat the oven to 350º F.
- Place cookware upside down on middle rack of oven and bake for 1 hour. Turn the oven off leaving the cookware in the oven until cool.

When finished the cookware will look slightly brown (instead of black), but it is seasoned and ready to use. To turn the cookware darker you may repeat the process 2 or 3 more times.

CARE FOR YOUR CAST IRON COOKWARE

Properly cared for cast iron cookware will last more than a lifetime. Here are some tips on maintaining your cookware for generations to enjoy:

CLEANING

After cooking in your cast iron cookware, clean the utensil with hot water and a stiff brush. Never use harsh detergents to clean iron as it will remove the seasoning.

Towel dry your cast iron thoroughly. While the utensil is still warm from the hot water wash, immediately wipe a light coat of PAM or vegetable oil on all cooking surfaces.

STORAGE

Store your cast iron in a cool, dry place. If you have a lid for the utensil, place a folded paper towel between the lid and the utensil to allow air to circulate, or store the lid elsewhere.

METALLIC TASTE OR SIGNS OF RUST

If you notice a metallic taste or your cookware shows signs of rust, simply scour off the rust, wash the cookware with soap and hot water, and re-season the cookware.

On the following pages you will notice
a series of silhouette icons of specific
cast iron cookware vessels. These icons
represent the recommended Lodge Cast
Iron pot or pan used to prepare the recipe.
Additionally, you will realize that some
recipes do not have an icon. These recipes
either call for a non-cast iron vessel, or
leave the specific utensil to your discretion.

Appetizers & Salads

It's true, there are not many salads made in cast iron. Nevertheless, in the South, it would come close to heresy to serve fried catfish and hush puppies without coleslaw. It is unlikely that there has ever been a church social without mounds of potato salad to accompany fried chicken. The cornbread salad recipes certainly demonstrate that one should never underestimate Southern ingenuity in discovering new ways to serve cornbread.

And who else but a Southerner, would have found yet another use for bacon grease by pouring it (with a little sugar and vinegar) over perfectly healthy salad greens, and viola – Wilted Lettuce Salad. Surely, the rest of the world must think that the four basic food groups of the South are salt, sugar, bacon grease, and beer!

CHILI PEPPER ARTICHOKE DIP

 Lodge 2 Qt.
Serving Pot

Taylor Watson
Chattanooga, Tennessee

1 can (14 oz.) artichokes, drained and chopped
2 cans (4 oz.) chopped green chilies, drained
1 cup mayonnaise
1 1/2 cups freshly grated Parmesan cheese, divided
Paprika for garnish

Preheat oven to 350° F. Mix all ingredients together, reserving some Parmesan cheese for topping. Put into serving pot. Sprinkle with reserved Parmesan cheese and paprika. Bake for 25 minutes until bubbling. Serve with crackers. I prefer Triscuits. The cast iron keeps the dip warm longer.

Serving Suggestions: Place pot on Lodge Baking Pan and surround with crackers.

SOUTHERN HOT ARTICHOKE DIP

 Lodge 2 Qt.
Serving Pot

Deena Gonce Brown

1 cup grated Parmesan cheese
1 package (8 oz.) Neufchatel cheese
1 cup light sour cream
1/8 teaspoon dry dill weed (fresh if you grow it)
1 can (13 3/4 oz.) artichoke hearts, drained and chopped
Crackers for dipping

Preheat oven to 325° F. Reserve 1 tablespoon of Parmesan cheese. Beat the remaining Parmesan, Neufchatel cheese, sour cream, and dill in a bowl with a mixer. Stir in chopped artichoke hearts. Spoon mixture into serving pot and sprinkle with reserved 1 tablespoon of Parmesan cheese. Bake uncovered for 30 minutes until lightly browned and hot in center. Makes 3 cups and stays good and hot in the cast iron. Leftovers should be taken out of cast iron and put in a plastic bowl with lid and stored in refrigerator. Use bandannas as napkins for a real country theme.

"My mother and both grandmothers have always used 2 or 3 cast iron skillets to prepare every meal."

BLACK-EYED PEA DIP
Christa Pesnell

 Lodge 2 Qt.
Serving Pot

1 can (15 oz.) black-eyed peas, drained
1 can (15 oz.) artichoke hearts, chopped and drained
1 small onion, finely chopped
2 tablespoons Parmesan cheese
1/2 cup mayonnaise
1 package Hidden Valley Ranch dressing mix
1 cup shredded Mozzarella cheese
Parsley flakes for garnish

Preheat oven to 350° F. Cut artichoke hearts into bite-size pieces. Mix all other ingredients together, except Mozzarella, and pour into serving pot. Top with Mozzarella cheese and sprinkle parsley flakes on top. Bake for 30 minutes. Serve with Frito Scoops.

CHIPPED BEEF DIP
Gayle Allen-Grier
Bob Kellermann's Executive Assistant (Retired)

 Lodge 2 Qt.
Serving Pot

1 package (8 oz.) cream cheese
2 tablespoons milk
1/2 cup sour cream
2 tablespoons dry onion flakes
1/2 tablespoon salt
1/8 teaspoon pepper
3 oz. chipped beef, shredded
1/2 cup Jalapeno peppers, chopped

Topping
1/2 cup pecans, chopped
1/2 teaspoon garlic salt
2 tablespoons butter or margarine

Preheat oven to 350° F. Soften cream cheese; stir in milk, sour cream, onion flakes, salt, pepper, beef, and peppers and mix well. Pour into serving pot. Heat pecans, garlic salt, and butter; mix and spread on top of mixture. Bake for 30 minutes. Serve hot with Frito Scoops.

PARTY MEATBALLS
Sarah Reed

 Lodge 2 Qt.
Serving Pot

1 pound ground beef
1 egg
1/4 cup evaporated milk
1/4 cup ketchup

1/2 cup cracker crumbs
1 medium onion, grated
Salt and pepper to taste

Sauce
1 bottle chili sauce
1 teaspoon lemon juice
1 cup grape jelly

Mix egg, milk, ketchup, and crackers. Set aside until crackers are soft. Add ground beef, onion, salt, and pepper. Mix well and shape into tiny balls. Heat chili sauce, lemon juice, and grape jelly to simmer in serving pot. Drop meatballs into simmering sauce. Cook until tender, about 30 minutes. Better made day before, cooled, and refrigerated in plastic storage bags. When ready to serve, reheat in serving pot to keep warm.

BLACK BEAN SALAD
Mary Miles Grider

4 cups black beans (fresh-cooked or canned)
1 medium red onion, minced
1 medium red Bell pepper, chopped
1 medium green Bell pepper, chopped
4 large Roma tomatoes, chopped
1/8 cup cilantro, minced
1/4 cup Feta cheese

Vinaigrette
1/2 cup olive oil
1/4 cup vinegar
Juice of 2 limes
Salt and pepper to taste

If using canned beans, rinse them before using. Place beans, onion, peppers, tomatoes, and cilantro in bowl. Crumble cheese into the mixture, and add vinaigrette dressing. Toss and refrigerate overnight before serving.

Put all dressing ingredients in a jar with a cover and shake well to mix.

COLESLAW WITH COOKED DRESSING

Faye Munn
Clarksville, Tennessee

8 cups cabbage, shredded
1 large onion, shredded
1 Bell pepper, shredded
1 cup sugar
1 cup cider vinegar

3/4 cup olive or salad oil
1 teaspoon prepared mustard
1 teaspoon celery seeds
1 teaspoon salt

Combine shredded cabbage, onion, and Bell pepper in a large glass or stainless bowl. Sprinkle with sugar; do not stir. Blend remaining ingredients in a saucepan and bring to a boil. Pour over cabbage; do not stir. Refrigerate overnight. This will keep a week or more if refrigerated. Serves 16.

CHINESE COLESLAW

Gayle Allen-Grier

1 package (10 oz.) shredded cabbage
1/2 cup green onion, chopped
1/4 cup Bell pepper, chopped
1 cup almonds, sliced or slivered
1/4 cup sesame seed
3 packages Ramen noodles

Dressing

1/4 cup sugar
2 tablespoons white vinegar
2 tablespoons soy sauce
1 cup salad oil
1 teaspoon pepper
3 flavor packets (from noodles)

Mix dressing ingredients and refrigerate. Preheat oven to 350° F. Crush noodles, mix with almonds and seeds and bake on cookie sheet 15 minutes. Mix cabbage, onion, and pepper and refrigerate. When ready to serve, combine all salad ingredients. Dressing can be added to entire mixture or to individual servings as desired.

STELLA'S CRANBERRY SALAD
Stella Harris

1 package fresh cranberries
1 2/3 cups sugar
1 cup chopped pecans
1 cup halved red grapes
1 small container of cool whip

Grind cranberries. Pour sugar over cranberries and let drain in colander for 8 hours. Discard juice. Mix remaining ingredients together, add cranberries and refrigerate.

Stella's granddaughter doesn't normally like cranberry salad, but said this one is delicious. "I could eat the whole bowl. I hope that you will try this one of Granny's."

POTATO SALAD
Charlotte Durham,
wife of Dallas who was with Lodge for 42 years

3 pounds potatoes
2 tablespoons finely chopped green onion
1/2 teaspoon dry mustard
1/2 teaspoon salt
1/2 teaspoon garlic salt
1/4 teaspoon sugar
Dash pepper
1/4 teaspoon Worcestershire sauce
2 tablespoons vinegar
6 tablespoons vegetable oil
2 boiled eggs, chopped
Sweet pickle cubes or relish to taste
16 ounces cottage cheese
1/2 cup mayonnaise

Cook potatoes in jackets in salted water. Peel and cut into pieces in large bowl and add onion. In a separate bowl, combine all spices, Worcestershire sauce, vinegar, and vegetable oil; pour over warm potatoes. Add pickle and eggs. Refrigerate for several hours or overnight. Thirty minutes before serving, combine cottage cheese and mayonnaise and add to potato mixture. Toss until blended.

WILTED LETTUCE SALAD
Bertha Russell Gonce

1 bunch leaf lettuce, torn (can also use spinach)
6 radishes, thinly sliced
4 to 6 green onions with tops, thinly sliced
4 boiled eggs

Dressing
5 bacon strips
2 tablespoons red wine vinegar
1 tablespoon lemon juice
1 teaspoon sugar
1/2 teaspoon pepper

Toss lettuce, radishes, and onions in a large bowl; set aside. In a skillet, cook bacon until crisp. Remove to paper towels to drain. To the hot drippings, add vinegar, lemon juice, sugar, and pepper; stir well. Immediately pour dressing over salad and toss gently. Crumble the bacon and slice the eggs and sprinkle on top.

This is a favorite springtime food of Marion and Bertha Gonce, who have farmed the Joseph Lodge farm since 1934. Bertha says it's the best when the lettuce, radishes, and onions are grown in your own garden and picked just before preparing.

CHILIE CORNBREAD SALAD

Lodge
8 In. Skillet

1 package (6 oz.) cornbread mix
1 can (4 oz.) chopped green chilies, drained
Pinch of sage
3 large tomatoes, chopped
1/2 cup green Bell pepper, chopped
1/2 cup green onions, chopped
1 package (1 oz.) Ranch salad dressing mix
1 cup sour cream
1 cup mayonnaise
2 cans (15 oz.) pinto beans, drained
2 cups Cheddar cheese, shredded
10 slices bacon, crisp-cooked and crumbled
2 cans (15 oz.) whole kernel golden sweet corn, drained

Prepare cornbread mix by directions on package, adding chilies and sage. Bake in skillet. Cool and crumble into mixing bowl. In a mixing bowl, combine tomatoes, green pepper, and green onions. In a separate bowl, combine the salad dressing mix, sour cream, and mayonnaise. In **a large** serving bowl, layer half of the cornbread crumbs, pinto beans, tomato mixture, cheese, bacon, corn, and salad dressing. Layer the remaining ingredients. Cover and refrigerate for at least 3 hours or overnight. Serves 20.

CHATTANOOGA CORNBREAD SALAD

Lodge
8 In. Skillet

1 skillet of cornbread, cooled
1/2 pound bacon, fried crisp and crumbled
2 medium Bell peppers, chopped
4 medium tomatoes, chopped
1/2 cup sweet pickles, chopped
Salt and pepper to taste

Dressing
1 cup mayonnaise
1/4 cup pickle juice
1 tablespoon sugar

Layer the ingredients in bowl beginning with crumbled cornbread, bacon, peppers, tomatoes, and pickles. Mix mayonnaise, pickle juice, and sugar and drizzle over top of cornbread mixture when ready to serve. Delicious after refrigerating overnight. Serves 10. Variation: 2 medium onions, chopped.

CORNBREAD SALAD
WITH BEANS

Lodge
Muffin Pan

1 box Jiffy corn muffin mix
2/3 cup mayonnaise
1/3 cup pickle juice, sweet or dill
1 can pinto beans, undrained
1 green pepper, chopped
1 small bunch green onions, chopped
1 tomato, chopped (you may want more)
1 pound bacon, fried crisp and crumbled
1 cup shredded Cheddar cheese

Prepare muffins according to instructions on box and cool. Mix mayonnaise and pickle juice together. Then layer ingredients of salad in serving dish as follows: 3 crumbled corn muffins, pinto beans, green pepper, green onion, and 3 remaining crumbled corn muffins. Top with mayonnaise mixture, tomatoes, bacon, and cheese. Cover and refrigerate for 3 to 4 hours or overnight. Serves 10.

PIMENTO CORNBREAD SALAD

Lodge
8 In. Skillet

1 skillet of buttermilk cornbread, cooled
1 large ripe tomato, diced
1 bunch scallions, tops and bottoms, finely chopped
2 stalks celery, finely chopped
1/2 cup lightly toasted and chopped pecans
1 Bell pepper, finely chopped
1 jar (3oz.) pimentos, drained and diced
Salt and pepper to taste
2 cups mayonnaise

Crumble cornbread in a large bowl. Stir in remaining ingredients, saving mayonnaise to last. Chill at least 1 hour before serving. Serves about 10.

Breads

Somewhere there exists an imaginary line that divides the North and the South more surely than the Mason-Dixon ever did. It is the division between cold rolls and hot biscuits.

Tradition usually begins with availability, and the soft-wheat flours available in the South did not bond well with yeast. When commercially prepared baking powder and baking soda became available to the Southern cook for leavening the soft flour, biscuits joined cornbread at the head of the table. Southern flour mills were soon packaging flour combined with just the right amount of baking powder and salt for making biscuits. This self-rising flour became known as "biscuit flour" in the South.

Few things are better than a hot, homemade, buttered biscuit – so good that Southern custom now dictates that be it biscuits, cornbread, or yeast rolls, it is almost illegal to serve bread that doesn't melt that slab of butter in 30 seconds or less.

BISCUIT TIPS

Personal preference dictates your choice of liquid. Buttermilk produces biscuits that are more moist with a sharper or tangier flavor than biscuits that are made with whole or "sweet" (as it is often referred to in the South) milk. If you're a novice at biscuit making, try both to determine your preference. Buttermilk is more acidic and requires baking powder and baking soda for the leavening agent, while "sweet" milk just requires baking powder.

- Cut the shortening into the dry ingredients until the mixture resembles coarse crumbs.

- When adding liquid ingredients to dry ingredients, mix quickly with a fork. Never use a mixer or food processor to mix or knead biscuit dough.

- As soon as the dough pulls away from the bowl, stop mixing. It is important not to over work biscuit dough.

- Turn dough onto lightly floured surface and knead only a few times, until the dough no longer feels sticky. Biscuit dough should not be overworked.

- Roll dough into a rectangle to your desired thickness. Do this by rolling up and down and side to side as few times as possible.

- Cut the biscuits close together, wasting as little dough as possible. You can pat the scraps together and re-cut, but those biscuits may not rise as high or be as pretty, but they still taste good!

- Don't use a twisting motion with the biscuit cutter, because the biscuits will not rise as high.

- For the best result, place biscuits on a greased cast iron skillet, griddle, or drop biscuit pan. If you like your biscuits with a crusty side, place them far apart so they will not touch when baking. If you prefer them with soft sides, place them on the pan barely touching.

- Bake in a preheated hot (450º F) oven.

- Butter while they are hot and enjoy!

BAKING POWDER BISCUITS

Carolyn Kellermann Millhiser

2 cups plain flour
2 teaspoons baking powder
1 teaspoon salt
3 tablespoons shortening
3/4 to 1 cup milk

Preheat oven to 450° F. Sift in dry ingredients, and work in the shortening with your fingers or a pastry cutter. Gradually add the milk, mixing it in with a spoon. The dough should be as soft as can be handled without sticking. Turn onto a lightly floured board, roll or pat lightly until 3/4 inch thick. Cut with floured biscuit cutter. (If you don't have a cutter, use a small can with both ends cut out.) Bake in a hot oven for about 15 minutes. Baking biscuits on cast iron gives the best end result.

"One of my most prized possessions is the biscuit cutter that my grandfather made from a Calumet baking powder can before my mother married in 1935."

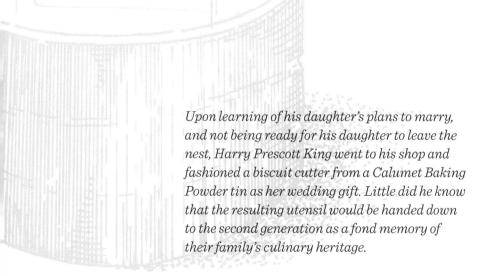

Upon learning of his daughter's plans to marry, and not being ready for his daughter to leave the nest, Harry Prescott King went to his shop and fashioned a biscuit cutter from a Calumet Baking Powder tin as her wedding gift. Little did he know that the resulting utensil would be handed down to the second generation as a fond memory of their family's culinary heritage.

BUTTERMILK BISCUITS

Lodge
Round Griddle

Gladys Ketner Padgett Tidman
granddaughter of the founder of Ketner's Mill

2 cups plain flour, sifted
1/4 teaspoon salt
1/2 teaspoon soda
2 teaspoons baking powder
4 level tablespoons vegetable shortening (Crisco)
1 cup buttermilk

Preheat oven to 450° F. In a large bowl, sift together the flour, salt, soda, and baking powder. Work in the shortening with your fingers or a pastry cutter. Stir in the buttermilk until just combined. Turn dough out onto a lightly floured board, roll or pat lightly until 1/2 inch thick and cut with a floured biscuit cutter. Place on preheated griddle and bake for about 10 minutes. This will make about 1 dozen biscuits, depending on size of the biscuit cutter.

Located in Marion County, Tennessee, just a stones throw from South Pittsburg, historic Ketner's Mill stands almost exactly as it did in the late 1800s. On the National Register of Historic Places in Marion County, the first annual fair was held in 1977 to commemorate a three year restoration of the mill. Until the death of Clyde Ketner in 1992, Ketner's was one of the last remaining daily operating grist mills in the country.

BUTTERMILK DROP BISCUITS

Lodge
Mini Cake Pan

Marilyn Geraldson

2 cups all-purpose flour
1 tablespoon baking powder
1/4 teaspoon baking soda
2 teaspoons sugar
1/2 teaspoon cream of tartar

1/4 teaspoon salt
1/2 cup butter, margarine or shortening
1 1/4 cups buttermilk

Preheat oven to 450° F. In a bowl, stir dry ingredients together. Cut in shortening with fork or pastry blender to coarse crumb stage. Add buttermilk. Stir until just blended. Drop dough into biscuit pan. Fill quite full. Bake about 30 minutes or until brown on top. Serve hot. Makes 7 biscuits.

Variation: Add 2 tablespoons finely shredded carrots, 1 tablespoon snipped parsley, and/or 1 tablespoon chopped green onion.

TOMATO GRAVY I

Lodge
10 1/4 In. Skillet

4 tablespoons shortening
Pepper to taste
1 onion, chopped
2 teaspoons unbleached flour
1 can (28 oz.) stewed tomatoes
Salt to taste

Heat shortening in skillet on high heat until just before it begins to smoke. Reduce heat to medium. Sprinkle pepper into skillet. Add chopped onion and cook until slightly done, stirring constantly with wooden spoon. Sprinkle flour over onion. Stir until flour begins to form a brown roux. Add tomatoes, undrained, stirring to blend with flour. Mash tomatoes as you continue to blend. Add water if it gets too thick. Add salt. Reduce heat to low and simmer until ready. Takes about 15 minutes. Serves about 4.

TOMATO GRAVY II

2 tablespoons canola oil
1/4 cup flour

Salt and pepper to taste
2 cups tomato juice

Brown flour in canola oil or bacon drippings along with salt and pepper to taste, stirring constantly. Add tomato juice. Cook until thickened. Serve over hot biscuits.

TOMATO GRAVY III

Small amount of bacon grease
2 ripe tomatoes from the garden
1 large Vidalia onion, chopped
Salt and pepper to taste
Dash Tabasco sauce
About 1/4 cup self-rising flour
1 or 2 cups of leftover coffee

Melt bacon grease in skillet and add finely chopped tomatoes. (Use the skillet that was just used to cook the breakfast bacon.) Heat the skillet on medium high. Add chopped onion and stir constantly, while adding salt, pepper, and Tabasco sauce and flour in sparing amounts. Cook until mixture thickens and then add 1 cup of coffee, still stirring constantly. Bring to a boil. Add a little more coffee as needed. Don't leave the mixture for a second. It will lump sure as can be! Serve over biscuits.

TENNESSEE CHOCOLATE GRAVY

Lodge
10 1/4 In. Skillet

Judy Maness
Dandridge, Tennessee

> 2 tablespoons butter or margarine
> 2 tablespoons cocoa
> 2 tablespoons flour
> 1/4 cup sugar
> 1/2 teaspoon vanilla
> 2 cups milk

Melt margarine or butter in skillet. Mix together dry ingredients. Add vanilla and milk to dry ingredients. (May mix better if put in clean mayonnaise jar with lid and shaken well.) Pour into skillet with melted butter and cook over medium-high heat, stirring constantly until thick. Serve with hot biscuits. Makes 2 cups.

GRANNY'S SAUSAGE AND GRAVY

Lodge
Combo Cooker

Vickie Davenport

> 1 pound pork sausage
> 1 1/2 tablespoons sausage drippings
> 3 tablespoons flour
> 1 1/2 cups milk
> Salt and pepper to taste

Crumble and brown sausage in large, deep skillet or bottom of Combo Cooker. Remove sausage and drain, leaving 1 to 1 1/2 tablespoons drippings in skillet. Sprinkle flour over fat. Cook on medium heat, stirring constantly until brown. Add milk, 1/2 cup at a time. Cook until gravy is thick. If you use the Combo Cooker, use the lid to bake your biscuits.

BLUSHING DROP BISCUITS

Youngie Plaster

Lodge
Mini Cake Pan

Sift together:
2 cups flour, sifted before measuring
2 1/2 teaspoons baking powder
1 teaspoon salt
1/3 cup shortening
1 cup tomato juice

Preheat oven to 450° F. Cut shortening into flour mixture until it resembles cornmeal. Add tomato juice to flour mixture. Drop from a spoon into a preheated drop biscuit pan, which has been sprayed well with Pam or Baker's Joy. Bake in the middle of oven for 15 minutes.

Variations: For bacon biscuits, add crumbled cooked bacon to mixture. For curried biscuits add 1/2 teaspoon curry powder to dry ingredients.

CHARLES' APPLE PANCAKES

Charles Cagle

Lodge 12 In.
Square Griddle

2 cups flour
1 tablespoon baking powder
1 teaspoon baking soda
2 teaspoons salt
3 tablespoons sugar
1 teaspoon cinnamon
2 1/4 cups sour milk or buttermilk
2 eggs, beaten
1 cup apples, peeled and cut in pieces
6 tablespoons butter, melted

Sift together flour, baking powder, baking soda, salt, sugar, and cinnamon. Beat milk and eggs in a small bowl. Add apples and melted butter. Add the milk mixture to the dry ingredients. Stir well. Cook as you would ordinary pancakes on a greased griddle. Brown on both sides. Serve plain or with butter and maple syrup.

BROTHER ANSELM'S POPOVERS

Brother Anselm Clark
O.S.B.

 Lodge
Muffin Pan

2 eggs
1 cup milk
1 cup plain flour
1/4 teaspoon salt
1 tablespoon butter, melted

Horseradish Sauce

1 cup sour cream
1/4 cup prepared Horseradish
1 green onion, chopped
1/4 teaspoon Texas Pete hot sauce
1/4 teaspoon salt
1/4 teaspoon pepper

Preheat oven to 425° F. Spray muffin pan with Baker's Joy. Heat greased muffin pan in oven for 10 minutes. Beat whole eggs until foamy. Add the milk and combine this mixture slowly with the sifted flour and salt. Beat just enough to mix well. Add melted butter. Pour into oiled and heated muffin pans, filling the sections 2/3 full. Bake 35 minutes or until brown. They should have hollow centers when they come out of the oven. Turn them upside down and make a split in the bottom. At the table, popovers are good with centers filled with jelly or gravy.

Variation: Add a dash of Worcestershire sauce and a pinch of dill weed to the batter. When popovers are done fill with Horseradish sauce, which has been made ahead of time and refrigerated.

Mix together all sauce ingredients and refrigerate until ready to serve. Fill popovers, bottom side up, through split made as popovers came out of oven. Serve hot.

Brother Clark was a monk with a baking background, trained at the Culinary Art Institute in New Haven, Connecticut. He resided at the Marion Mission for several years across the Tennessee River from South Pittsburg. His weekly bread baking came to be greatly anticipated by all. He offered this recipe to be used with Lodge bakeware for your enjoyment.

AEBLESKIVER (PANCAKE BALLS)

Sarah Kirkwood Lodge
affectionately called "Pat"

Aebleskiver
Pan

4 eggs, separated
1 tablespoons sugar
2 cups cake flour
1/2 teaspoon salt

1 teaspoon baking powder
1/4 cup shortening, melted
Scant 2 cups milk

Beat egg yokes until lemon colored. Sift together the dry ingredients and add alternately with shortening and milk. Fold in stiffly beaten egg whites. Place a small amount of shortening or oil in each cup of Aebleskiver pan and fill 2/3 full with batter. Cook over medium heat until bubbly; turn carefully with knitting needles or fork and finish browning other side. Turn each one over several times during baking to ensure thorough baking. Serve with syrup, jam, or jelly or sprinkle with powdered sugar.

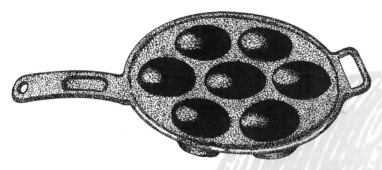

FANCY PANCAKE

Pauline Clepper

Lodge
Round Griddle

3 eggs
1/2 cup milk
1/2 cup flour
1/4 cup sugar
1/2 teaspoon salt
1 tablespoon butter
1 tablespoon confectioner's sugar to dust on top

Preheat oven to 400° F. Beat eggs, milk, flour, sugar, and salt together. In griddle, melt butter in oven. Pour the egg batter onto the hot griddle and place back in the oven. Bake 10 minutes or until pancake is light brown. When done, sift sugar over the top and serve while hot. Good topped with fruit or a sauce. Serves 4.

DANISH AEBLESKIVER

Claude Teisen-Simony
Frederiksburg, Denmark

2 cups flour, sifted
2 tablespoons sugar
1 teaspoon baking soda
1 teaspoon cardamom
3/4 teaspoon salt
1 cup sour cream
2/3 cup milk
3 egg yolks, beaten
3 egg whites, beaten
2 tablespoons butter, melted
1 tablespoon butter, melted or vegetable oil for greasing wells

Set Aebleskiver pan on stove burner on low heat. Sift dry ingredients together and set aside. In smaller bowl, combine sour cream, milk, egg yolks, and melted butter. Make a well in center of dry ingredients and add liquid mixture, stirring until well blended. Gently fold beaten egg whites into batter. Test Aebleskiver by dropping a few drops of cold water into the pan. If drops dance around in small beads, temperature is right. Add about 1/2 teaspoon melted butter or vegetable oil into wells and heat. Pour batter into wells, filling 1/2 to 2/3 full. With knitting needles or fork, turn pancake balls frequently to brown evenly. Do not pierce. Pancake balls are done when a wooden pick inserted in center comes out clean. Serve immediately sprinkled with confectioner's sugar. If desired, accompany with a tart jam. Makes about 4 dozen balls.

Variation: Rinse, pare, and dice 2 medium-size apples. Sprinkle about 1 teaspoon of diced apples over batter in each well while cooking.

"Aebleskive" means "apple slice" in Danish. The original aebleskivers always contained apples."

CREPES SUZETTE

Jayne Clepper Halvorson

Lodge
6 In. Skillet

Lodge 10 1/4 In.
Skillet (Sauce)

3 eggs
1 cup all-purpose flour, sifted
Salt to taste
1 cup water
Canola oil for the skillet
1/2 teaspoon vanilla

Sauce
6 tablespoons butter
3 tablespoons sugar
Peel and juice of one orange
Fresh fruit, chopped

In a mixing bowl, beat eggs and gradually add the flour, mixing well. Add salt and water, beating to make a light smooth batter. Heat the 6 inch skillet on medium heat. Brush with canola oil and add two tablespoons of batter at a time. Cook the crepes on one side only until they are set; do not brown them. It takes about one minute. When they are done, transfer to a piece of wax paper. They can be frozen until ready to use.

In a 10 1/4 inch skillet, melt the butter with the sugar, orange peel and juice. Cook until sugar is dissolved. Fold the prepared crepes in quarters and add a few at a time into the butter and sugar mixture. Spoon the sauce over the crepes until they are hot. It will take a minute or two. Serve with fresh fruit garnish.

THE STORY OF CREPE SUZETTE

One day Henri Charpentier was composing a crepe sauce for his patron Albert, Prince of Wales. By accident the liquor caught fire and Henri feared a culinary disaster. Not having time to start the recipe over, and with thoughts of becoming the first executed French chef, he served the waiting Prince.

The Prince tasted the sauce, and asked what the fabulous cakes were called. Henri, hoping to improve his accidental fortune, quickly exclaimed, "Crepes Princesse." Acknowledging the compliment, Prince Albert pointed out the presence of a small girl; and Henri graciously consented to rename his creation Crepe Suzette.

ST. GEORGE ISLAND BUTTERMILK PANCAKES

John Richard Lodge, Jr.

Lodge Reversible
Grill/Griddle

1 1/4 cups unbleached flour
1 tablespoon sugar
2 teaspoons baking powder
1/2 teaspoon baking soda

1/2 teaspoon salt
2 large eggs, beaten
1 1/2 cups buttermilk
2 tablespoons corn oil

Whisk or sift dry ingredients together. In separate bowl, mix eggs, buttermilk, and oil. Stir into dry ingredients until just mixed. Pour onto hot griddle by large spoonful. Cook first side until pancake bubbles and dries slightly on edge, flip and finish cooking. Serve with butter and honey.

"Dick", great grandson of Joseph Lodge (founder of Lodge) and grandson of Leslie Lodge (second president of Lodge), is an attorney by vocation and a cook by avocation and member of Lodge Board of Directors since 1973.

QUICK APPLESAUCE MUFFINS

Betty Thomas

2 Lodge
Muffin Pan

2 cups Bisquick mix
1/4 cup sugar
1 teaspoon cinnamon
1/2 cup applesauce
1/4 cup milk
1 egg, lightly beaten
2 tablespoons canola oil
1/4 cup chopped walnuts or pecans

Put greased muffin pans in oven and heat to 400° F. Combine Bisquick with sugar and cinnamon. Add applesauce, milk, egg, oil, and nuts and beat well for 30 seconds. Fill hot muffin pans 2/3 full. Bake 12 minutes or until lightly browned. Cool for 10-15 minutes and take out of muffin pan. Spread with melted butter and sprinkle with cinnamon sugar. The muffins will slip right out of the well-seasoned cast iron if it is sprayed with Baker's joy and the pan is hot when you add the batter. Makes 12-14 muffins.

BRAN MUFFINS
Sarah Kirkwood Lodge

Lodge
Muffin Pan

3 cups sugar
5 cups flour
1 box (15 oz.) raisin bran cereal
5 teaspoons baking soda
1 teaspoon salt

4 eggs, slightly beaten
1 quart buttermilk
2 sticks butter or margarine, melted
Raisins or chopped nuts

Preheat oven to 400° F. Generously grease muffin pan. Mix dry ingredients together in a very large bowl. In separate bowl, mix wet ingredients together. Fold wet mixture into the dry mixture. Fill muffin pan 2/3 full. Bake 20 minutes until done. Place remaining batter in tightly covered container. Will keep in refrigerator for about two months. Makes about 48 muffins.

BERTHA'S CARROT-ZUCCHINI MUFFINS
Bertha Russell Gonce

Lodge
Muffin Pan

1 cup all purpose flour
1 cup whole wheat flour
1/2 cup sugar
1 teaspoon baking powder
1 teaspoon ground cinnamon
1/2 teaspoon salt

1/2 teaspoon baking soda
1 egg, beaten
3/4 cup orange juice
1/4 cup butter, melted
2 medium carrots, shredded
1 medium zucchini, shredded

Preheat oven to 400° F. Combine first 7 dry ingredients in a large bowl. In another bowl, stir together egg, orange juice, and butter; add to dry ingredients, stirring just until moistened. Fold in carrots and zucchini. Spoon into greased muffin pans, filling 2/3 full. Bake for 20 minutes. Remove from pans immediately, and cool on wire racks. Very good topped with a cream cheese frosting. Makes 18-24 muffins.

HAM AND SAUSAGE MUFFINS
Martha Holland

 Lodge
Muffin Pan

3 tablespoons butter
1/2 cup finely chopped green pepper
1/2 cup finely chopped green onions
1 cup finely chopped ham
1 cup finely chopped cooked sausage
1 cup yellow cornmeal
1 1/4 cups flour
2 teaspoons baking soda
1 teaspoon salt
2 eggs
2 cups buttermilk

Preheat oven to 400° F. In a cast iron skillet, melt butter and sauté green pepper and onions until soft, but not brown. In a large bowl, sift cornmeal, flour, soda, and salt. In a smaller bowl, beat eggs and stir in buttermilk. Add egg mixture to flour mixture all at once, stirring only until blended. Do not over stir. Carefully fold in ham, sausage, green pepper, and onions with any butter left in skillet. Spoon into well greased muffin pans, filling 2/3 full. Bake for 30 minutes until nicely browned. Makes 24 muffins.

Tip: To freeze, seal cooled muffins in plastic bags. Before serving, thaw in bags about 15 minutes. Remove from bags and wrap tightly in foil and heat in 400° F oven about 15 minutes.

YELLOW SQUASH MUFFINS

Debbie Clepper Pickens

 Lodge
Muffin Pan

> *2 cups cooked squash (about 8 medium size squash)*
> *2 eggs*
> *1 cup butter, melted*
> *1 cup sugar*
> *3 cups flour*
> *2 scant tablespoons baking powder*
> *1 teaspoon salt*

Wash squash and slice, after trimming off the ends. Cook in boiling water for 15 minutes or until tender. Drain and mash squash. Preheat oven to 375° F. Grease and heat muffin pans. If you don't have several, you will need to cook in batches. Combine squash, eggs, and butter; mix well and set aside. In another bowl, combine the dry ingredients and add the squash mixture, stirring lightly. Spoon batter into hot greased muffin pans, filling 3/4 full. Bake on bottom rack for 15 minutes or until brown on top. You can test with toothpick. Makes about 18 muffins, depending on size of muffin pans.

APPLESAUCE LOAF CAKE

 2 Lodge
Loaf Pans

> *1 1/2 cup unsweetened applesauce*
> *1 egg*
> *1 cup sugar*
> *2 tablespoons butter, melted*
> *1 teaspoon vanilla*
> *2 cups all-purpose flour*
> *2 teaspoons baking soda*
> *1/2 teaspoon cinnamon*
> *1/2 teaspoon cloves*
> *1/4 teaspoon nutmeg*
> *1 cup raisins*
> *1 cup chopped walnuts*

Preheat oven to 350° F. In large bowl, combine first 5 ingredients. Sift together flour, baking soda, cinnamon, cloves, and nutmeg. Add to applesauce mixture and mix well. Stir in raisins and walnuts. Pour into 2 greased loaf pans. Bake for 45-55 minutes. Cool for 10 minutes. Serves 12-16.

MOIST BANANA NUT BREAD

Nancy Ballard

2 Lodge
Loaf Pans

1 stick of margarine or butter
2 eggs
1 1/2 cups sugar
2 medium ripe bananas, mashed
1 teaspoon vanilla
1 1/2 cups self-rising flour
1 teaspoon baking soda
3/4 cups walnuts
1/2 cups raisins

Preheat oven to 325° F. In large bowl, mix all ingredients in above order, by hand. Pour batter into 2 greased loaf pans. Bake for 1 hour. Will be nice and brown. Cool 10-15 minutes and remove bread from loaf pan. Delicious bread. Wrap in aluminum foil. Will keep in the refrigerator for a week or two.

MARY FLORENCE'S LEMON BREAD

Mary Florence Padgett Smith

Lodge
Loaf Pan

1/3 cup butter, melted
1 cup sugar, divided
2 eggs, lightly beaten
1 1/2 cups flour
1/2 cup milk
1 1/2 teaspoons baking powder
1 teaspoon salt
1/2 cup chopped nuts
Rind of one lemon, grated
Juice of one lemon

Preheat oven to 350° F. Combine all ingredients except for lemon juice and 1/3 cup sugar. Blend well and pour into buttered and floured loaf pan, filling 2/3 full. Bake for 50-60 minutes. While the bread is still warm, combine the reserved lemon juice and 1/3 cups of sugar. Punch several holes in loaf with a toothpick. Pour lemon/sugar mixture over the top of the loaf. Let the bread cool in the pan. Freezes well.

DEBBIE'S POPPY SEED BREAD

Debbie Clepper Pickens

 3 Lodge
Loaf Pans

3 cups flour
2 1/4 cups sugar
1 1/2 teaspoons baking powder
1 1/2 teaspoons salt
3 eggs
1 1/8 cups oil
1 1/2 cups milk
1 1/2 tablespoons poppy seeds

Glaze

1/2 cup sugar
1/4 cup orange juice
1 1/2 teaspoons of vanilla
1 1/2 teaspoons almond extract
1 1/2 teaspoons butter flavoring

Preheat oven to 350° F. Mix all bread ingredients in a large bowl.
Beat 2 minutes with mixer. Divide dough into loaf pans. Bake for 1
hour. Pour glaze over hot bread when it is done.

BEER ROLLS

Youngie Plaster

 Lodge
Muffin Pan

3 cups Bisquick
3 tablespoons sugar
1 can (12 oz.) beer

Preheat oven to 375° F. Put well-greased (or sprayed with Baker's
Joy) muffin pans in preheated oven to heat. Blend together
Bisquick, sugar, and beer. Spoon into hot muffin pans. Bake until
brown. Makes 12-14 muffins.

GRAMMA'S BREAD

Edith Lodge Kellermann's recipe
as written by Lynda King Kellermann for her children

1/2 cup lukewarm water
1 package (1/4 oz.) dry yeast
4 1/2 cups flour, sifted and then measured
2 tablespoons sugar, rounded
2 tablespoons shortening (Crisco), rounded
1 teaspoon salt, heaping or rounded
1 1/2 cups milk, scalded

Sprinkle dry yeast on lukewarm water and set aside to dissolve and swell. Put sugar, salt, and shortening in a large mixing bowl. Scald the milk by heating it in saucepan until tiny bubbles form around the edge of the pan and the milk reaches about 180° F. Pour the milk over the sugar, salt, and shortening. When the milk melts the shortening, stir and let cool to lukewarm. Stir in flour and yeast mixture being sure to scrape down the sides of the bowl. Spread a dry clean dish towel over the bowl, put a lid on to make it airtight, and then wrap the bowl in a heavy towel. Set aside in a draft free spot and allow dough to rise until it doubles in size. Makes two loaves. Grease two loaf pans with shortening. If the pans are too cold, warm them to help melt the shortening. Let pans cool to lukewarm.

Kneading the dough: Place dough on floured breadboard. Work down with floured hands to get the air out of the dough. Fold the dough toward you, push it or slap it down with the back of your palm.

When the dough is firm, cut in half, and roll each half towards you to form an oblong loaf. Put into greased pans and turn once so the top-side is greased. Cover with cloth. Let rise about 30 or 40 minutes. Preheat oven to 500° F. Turn oven back to 400° F and put the bread in. Bake at 400° F first 10 minutes, cut oven back to 350° F, and bake 20 minutes longer. Turn loaves over in the pans. Bake another 30 minutes. Total baking time will be about an hour. Tip: Watch your oven temperature. You may have to turn your oven back to 325° F or 300° F for the last 30 minutes.

Edith (the only daughter of Joseph Lodge) made this bread daily for her family of 5 boys and 2 girls, ordering Kansas winter wheat flour in 50 pound bags. She filled her sifter with winter wheat flour and sifted in without measuring.

SPOON ROLLS

Sarah Kirkwood Lodge
Billie Cline Hill

 Lodge
Mini Cake Pan

1 package (1/4 oz.) dry yeast
2 cups lukewarm water
1/4 cup sugar

1 egg, beaten
3/4 cups butter, melted
4 cups self-rising flour

Preheat oven to 400° F. Dissolve yeast in warm water and let it
sit for yeast to swell. Mix in remaining ingredients. Spoon batter
into well-greased drop biscuit pan or muffin pan until 1/2 to 2/3
full. Bake for 20 minutes. Unused batter can be kept in refrigerator
in covered container for a week. Makes about 14 rolls.

QUICK ROLLS

Helen Clay

 Lodge
10 1/4 In. Skillet

3 cups flour
1 rounded teaspoon salt
2 level teaspoons baking powder
1/2 level teaspoon baking soda
2 level teaspoons sugar
1 cup buttermilk
1 cake Fleischmann's yeast, dissolved in 1/2 cup lukewarm water
2 tablespoons rounded shortening, melted and cooled

Preheat oven to 425° F. Mix all dry ingredients together. Add liquid
and shortening and more flour (if necessary) for stiffer dough.
Roll out as biscuits and let rise in warm room for 1 hour. Place in
large, well-greased skillet. Bake for 12 minutes until brown on top.

*Helen Clay offers this recipe in fond memory of Anna
Blackmon Dean (born 1868) with the following story:
Grace Dean Havron, teacher of Latin and English at South
Pittsburg High School from the 1930s until the 1950s, once
took her student, Fredrick Clay, to assist her mother with
some chores at the home place in Wartrace, Tennessee. That
day, Mrs. Dean insisted on preparing lunch for all. Fredrick
Clay liked these rolls so much that he asked for the recipe
for his mother. Mrs. Fanny Clay prepared these rolls for her
family until her death in 1968. Since the recipe was created
in the days of the wood stove, Mrs. Clay had to determine
oven temperature and minutes for her electric oven.*

Cornbread

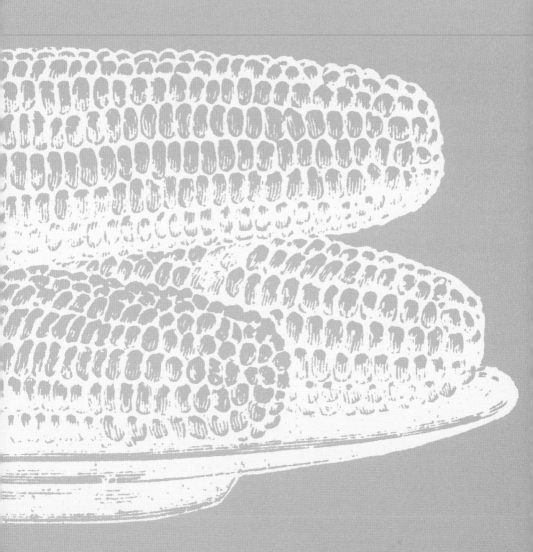

Though corn is North America's indigenous grain, and cornbread was America's first bread, it was the South that made cornbread an art form. Perhaps this is because nothing is better for sopping up every drop of soup or stew or the "pot likker" from the bottom of a bowl of greens. Today cornbread is still available at most every meal, and it is as much a part of us as our drawl. We could not imagine losing it anymore than we could imagine losing Magnolia trees or ice (no "d") tea. Cornbread is not simply intertwined with us: it IS us.

However, cornbread is not the same thing in the South as it is in the rest of the United States. As a matter of fact, about the only things these two breads have in common are cornmeal and the total look of astonishment shared by the Northerner who bites into Southern cornbread and the Southerner who bites into Northern cornbread for the very first time. Southern cornbread is ALWAYS made in cast iron from white cornmeal, and for the purist, has little, if any sugar or flour. The rest of the country likes cornbread made from yellow cornmeal with lots of sugar and flour, and from a Southern point of view, should be served for dessert.

For cornbread lovers, the debate still rages.

ELIZABETH'S BASIC CORNBREAD

Elizabeth Rogers Kelly

Lodge
10 1/4 In. Skillet

1 cup white self-rising cornmeal
1 egg
Enough buttermilk to make batter very thin (about 1 cup)

Put the greased pan into oven and heat as oven preheats to 450° F. Mix the batter: Pour batter into hot skillet. Bake for 20 minutes or until nicely browned.

ELIZABETH'S SCALDED CORNBREAD

Elizabeth Adams

Lodge
10 1/4 In. Skillet

2 cups white cornmeal
1/2 cup boiling water
1 teaspoon baking soda
1/2 teaspoon salt
2 or 3 eggs, beaten
1 tablespoon bacon grease or vegetable oil
1 cup buttermilk

Put 1 or 2 tablespoons of oil into skillet and put it in oven while preheating to 400° F. Meanwhile scald the cornmeal with boiling water. Stir to cool and to avoid lumping. Add buttermilk gradually to scalded cornmeal. Add beaten eggs, baking soda, salt, and mix well with spoon. Remove skillet from oven and pour hot oil into batter and stir. Then pour batter into hot skillet so that a brown, crisp crust will form. Bake 25 minutes, or until brown.

"This is an old family recipe from Tunica, Mississippi."

Elizabeth has many pieces of cast iron that she uses everyday, but her favorites are the two pieces that were the only things left after their house burned down 35 years ago.

JODY'S REAL CORNBREAD

Lodge
9 In. Skillet

Jody McDowell
Clinton Township, Michigan

> 2 eggs, beaten
> 1/2 teaspoon baking soda
> 2 cups buttermilk
>
> 2 cups white self-rising cornmeal
> 2 tablespoons bacon grease
> (or vegetable oil)

Preheat oven to 450° F. Place both tablespoons of fat of choice in skillet (bacon grease tastes the best, but vegetable oil or shortening works with a little added salt). Put skillet in oven to preheat. Combine cornmeal, baking soda, eggs, and buttermilk in bowl. Whisk together until well blended. Carefully remove hot skillet from oven and pour grease from skillet into batter. Pour batter into skillet, which will sizzle and may splatter. Bake for 30-40 minutes until golden brown. Remove from oven and let cool about 5-10 minutes. Then turn out onto plate so the bread is upside down, revealing crispy brown crust. With very sharp knife, cut into 6 or 8 wedges, and serve hot with lots of butter. If you like a crunchier texture, sprinkle some cornmeal into hot skillet before adding batter.

"I make this when I have Yankee guests for dinner."

MARTHA HOLLAND'S CORNBREAD

Lodge
Wedge Pan

Martha Holland

> 2 tablespoons bacon grease or vegetable oil
> 1 1/2 cups white self-rising cornmeal
> 1/2 teaspoon baking soda
> 1 cup buttermilk
> 2 eggs
> Black pepper and salt to taste

Put oil or grease in skillet and put in oven while preheating to 500° F. Mix remaining ingredients together and beat about 30 strokes with spoon. Remove hot skillet from oven and pour the hot oil or bacon grease into batter and beat some more. Pour batter into hot skillet and return to oven. Bake for 15 minutes. This recipe produces a crispier crust in a wedged skillet.

Martha says that the secret to good cornbread is using fresh buttermilk and a good beating.

MAYONNAISE
CORNBREAD FOR TWO

Charles Cagle

1 tablespoon bacon grease
1/4 cup white self-rising cornmeal
1/4 cup self-rising flour
2 tablespoons mayonnaise
1/2 cup milk
1 egg, slightly beaten (optional)

Preheat oven and skillet with bacon grease to 450° F. Combine cornmeal, flour, mayonnaise, and milk together. Beat egg into batter, if desired. Remove hot skillet from oven and pour hot grease into batter and stir. Pour batter into skillet. Bake for about 15 minutes until top is lightly brown.

Charles Cagle says, that when the oil begins to smoke you know the skillet is hot enough. You can also test it with a drop of water that sizzles when dropped on skillet. Charles always liked to crumble hot cornbread into a glass of milk, sit down, and enjoy.

COUNTRY MILKSHAKE
OR CORNBREAD SMOOTHIE

Charles Cagle

Take one tall ice tea glass. Crumble cornbread, filling glass to the top with sweet milk or buttermilk. Eat with ice tea spoon.

CORNBREAD REGIONS AT A GLANCE

INGREDIENTS	SOUTH	SOUTHWEST	REST OF U.S.
Cornmeal	White	Yellow	Yellow
Flour	None to Very Little	Some	Lots
Sugar	None to Very Little	None to Very Little	Lots
Pan	Cast Iron	Baking Pan	Baking Pan or Muffin Pan

CORN LIGHT BREAD
Patsy Barker Beene

Lodge
10 1/4 In. Skillet

4 tablespoons shortening or bacon grease
2 cups white cornmeal
1/2 cup flour
1/2 cup sugar
2/3 teaspoon baking soda
2 teaspoon baking powder
1 teaspoon salt
2 cups buttermilk

Put skillet with shortening into oven while preheating the oven to 350° F. Sift all dry ingredients together. Add buttermilk. Remove hot skillet from oven and pour hot shortening into batter. Pour batter into hot skillet. Bake for about 1 hour.

"I made this for my daughters' church youth group. The teenagers topped slices of hot bread with barbecue."

CRACKLIN' CORNBREAD
June Chance

Lodge
10 1/4 In. Skillet

1 or 2 tablespoons vegetable oil
2 cups white self-rising cornmeal
1 egg, beaten
1/2 cup cracklings
1 cup buttermilk (maybe more)

Heat oil in skillet while oven is preheating to 425° F. Leave skillet longer if necessary to make it very hot. Mix remaining ingredients. Remove hot skillet from oven and pour batter into hot skillet. Bake until firm and slightly brown on top, about 30 minutes.

Cracklings are diced salt pork, which has been cooked until all the fat has been rendered. They can be purchased at most grocery stores. The cook's preference is Hormel brand.

CORNSTICKS

Faye Marsh

Lodge
Cornstick Pan

1 tablespoon shortening for greasing pan
1 tablespoon shortening for batter, melted in Melting Pot
1 1/2 cups white cornmeal
1/2 cup flour
1 teaspoon salt
2 teaspoons baking powder
1/2 teaspoon baking soda
1 egg
1 cup buttermilk
1/4 cup water

Grease cornstick pans with shortening, place in oven and heat while oven preheats to 450° F. Mix cornmeal, flour, salt, soda, and baking powder. Then add egg and buttermilk and beat with spoon. Add melted shortening and enough water to make a thin batter. Remove cornstick pan or pans from oven (be sure that pans are very hot) and fill each stick 2/3 full. Bake until slightly brown on top, about 15 minutes. Makes about 15 cornsticks. Thin batter, hot cast iron pans, and hot oven are the secrets to good cornsticks.

CORNBREAD STICKS

Norma R. Neperud

Lodge
Cornstick Pan

2 tablespoons shortening, divided
1 cup white cornmeal
3 tablespoons flour
1/2 teaspoon salt
1 teaspoon baking powder
1/4 teaspoon baking soda
1 cup buttermilk
1 egg, beaten

Use 1 tablespoon shortening to grease cornstick pan or pans and place in oven as it preheats to 475° F. Combine dry ingredients. In separate bowl, combine buttermilk and egg, mixing well. Add wet mixture to dry ingredients and mix well. Melt 1 tablespoon shortening in melting pot and stir into batter. Remove very hot cornstick pan from oven and spoon batter into pan, filling 2/3 full. Bake for 12 to 15 minutes until slightly brown on top. Makes 11 cornsticks.

AUNT JIMMIE'S YEAST CORNBREAD

Jimmie Russell

Lodge 10 1/2 In. Square Skillet

1/2 cup corn oil
1 cup white self-rising cornmeal
1 cup self-rising flour
1/2 teaspoon baking soda
1 package dry yeast
1 egg
1 1/2 cups buttermilk

Preheat oven to 400° F. Put oil into skillet and place in oven to heat. Combine all ingredients in mixing bowl. Stir until well blended. Remove skillet from oven and pour the hot oil from skillet into mixture and stir. Pour mixture back into hot skillet and bake for about 20 minutes until brown on top. Flip bread onto platter and serve hot with butter.

GAYNELLE'S YEAST CORN LIGHT BREAD

Gaynelle Jacobs Grider

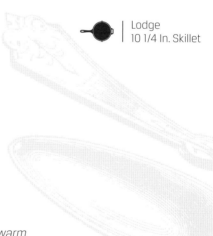

Lodge 10 1/4 In. Skillet

2 cups white cornmeal
1 cup flour
1/2 teaspoon salt
1/4 cup sugar
1 teaspoon baking powder
1/2 teaspoon baking soda
1 package active dry yeast
1/4 cup butter
2 1/2 cups buttermilk, heated to lukewarm

In skillet, over low heat, melt the butter, tilting and rotating the skillet to allow the butter to coat the sides. Set the skillet aside to cool. In a medium mixing bowl, stir together the dry ingredients, including the yeast. Add the lukewarm buttermilk and stir to blend. (The buttermilk should only be lukewarm so not to kill the yeast). Pour the batter into prepared skillet. Cover the skillet and set aside in a warm, draft-free place for the batter to rise (about 30 minutes). Preheat oven to 350° F and bake for 30 minutes, or until it is golden brown. This bread is good hot or cold.

BROCCOLI BREAD

Helen Fannelle Clay

Lodge 10 1/2 In.
Square Skillet

1 stick margarine or butter
1 box frozen chopped broccoli, thawed and drained
1 can (8 oz.) Mexi-corn
1 onion, chopped
6 ounces cottage cheese
3/4 teaspoon salt
4 eggs, beaten
1 box Jiffy Corn Muffin Mix

Put margarine in skillet and heat as oven preheats to 450° F. Mix remaining ingredients. Remove skillet from oven and pour melted margarine into batter and stir. Pour batter into hot skillet. Bake for about 30 minutes, until slightly brown on top. Let cool about 10 minutes and invert onto plate. The square cornbread looks good and cuts nicely into servings. Serve hot with butter.

SOUR CREAM CORNBREAD

Emma Rogers Thomas
Christine Rogers

Lodge
9 In. Skillet

1/2 cup vegetable oil, divided
1 can (8oz.) cream-style corn
1 cup sour cream
1 cup white self-rising cornmeal
3 eggs, beaten
1/4 teaspoon salt or seasoning salt, or to taste

Place 1/4 cup oil in skillet and heat while oven preheats to 400° F. Thoroughly mix the remainder of oil with the rest of the ingredients. Remove skillet from oven and pour batter into hot skillet. Bake 45 minutes, or until lightly brown on top.

ULTIMATE CORNBREAD
Virginia Loyd

Lodge
10 1/4 In. Skillet

1/4 cup vegetable oil
2 cups chopped onion
1/4 cup margarine or butter
8 ounces sour cream
1 cup shredded Cheddar cheese, divided
1 1/2 cups white self-rising cornmeal
1 tablespoon sugar
1/4 teaspoon dill weed
2 eggs, beaten
1 can (8 oz.) cream-style corn
1/4 cup milk
Dash of hot sauce

Put vegetable oil into skillet and place in oven while preheating to 375° F. To prepare topping, sauté onions in another skillet in margarine until tender and let cool. Then stir in sour cream and 1/2 cup cheese. Set aside. In separate bowl, mix remaining ingredients together. Remove skillet from oven and pour hot oil into batter and stir. Spoon batter into hot skillet. Spread sour cream mixture over top and sprinkle with remaining cheese. Bake for 35-40 minutes until done.

VIDALIA CORNBREAD
Carolyn Gonce LeRoy

Lodge
9 In. Skillet

2 cups white self-rising cornmeal
1 tablespoon sugar
1 teaspoon baking powder
1 egg, slightly beaten
2 tablespoons vegetable oil
2 cups milk
2 cups finely chopped Vidalia onions

Preheat oven to 350° F. Combine all ingredients except onions (batter will be thin). Stir in onions, mixing well. Pour into a well-greased skillet. Bake for 40 minutes or until golden brown. Let cool 10 minutes before serving. Serves 8.

ZUCCHINI CORNBREAD

Carolyn Gonce LeRoy

Lodge
9 In. Skillet

3 cups grated zucchini
1/2 teaspoon salt
1 stick butter, melted
1/2 cup sour cream
1 onion, grated
2 tablespoons sugar
4 eggs, slightly beaten
1 1/2 cups white self-rising cornmeal

Grate zucchini into colander and sprinkle with the salt. Let stand 10 minutes. Drain. Preheat oven to 350° F. Spray skillet with nonstick vegetable oil spray. Combine all ingredients except cornmeal. Add the cornmeal and stir until well mixed. Pour into skillet and bake for 45 minutes or until brown.

"This recipe was handed down from my mother, Bertha Gonce."

BLACK SKILLET CORNBREAD

Charles Cagle

Lodge
10 1/4 In. Skillet

1 cup fine white cornmeal
1 cup flour
1 tablespoon sugar
2 teaspoons baking powder
1/2 teaspoon baking soda
Dash of salt
1 egg, beaten
1 cup buttermilk
1/2 cup frozen corn, thawed
1 cup Cheddar cheese, grated
2 pickled Jalapenos, minced
4 tablespoons butter, melted

Preheat oven to 375° F. Grease skillet. In a large bowl combine cornmeal, flour, sugar, baking powder, baking soda, and salt. Mix together the egg and the buttermilk. Stir buttermilk mixture into dry ingredients. Add corn, 2/3 cup Cheddar cheese and minced Jalapenos. Stir in melted butter and mix gently. Pour batter into prepared skillet and top with remaining Cheddar cheese. Bake for 20-25 minutes or until inserted knife comes out clean. Let cool for 5 minutes and remove from skillet to a cooling rack.

AZTEC BREAD

Lodge
9 In. Skillet

Pat Sparkman, Knoxville, Tennessee
Pat is the wife of Frank Sparkman, the architect
for the South Pittsburg Princess Theatre restoration

1/2 cup butter, melted
1 jar (4 oz.) chopped pimentos
2 eggs, slightly beaten
1/4 cup buttermilk
1 cup white self-rising cornmeal
1 can (8 oz.) cream-style corn
6 ounces sharp Cheddar cheese, cubed
1 can (4 oz.) chopped chilies

Put butter in skillet and place in oven while preheating to 400° F.
Beat eggs and buttermilk together. Add remaining ingredients
and mix well. Remove skillet from oven and pour butter into batter
and stir. Pour batter into the heated skillet. Bake 45 minutes or
until done. Enjoy while hot.

KATE'S MEXICAN CORNBREAD

2 Lodge
Muffin Pans

Kate McCuiston

1 1/2 cups white self-rising cornmeal
1/2 onion, chopped
1/2 cup vegetable oil
1/2 cup chopped Bell pepper
2 eggs, beaten
1 cup sour cream
1 can (8 oz.) cream-style corn

Use some of the oil to generously grease the muffin pan. Put pan
in oven while oven is preheating to 450° F. Mix all ingredients
together including the remaining oil. Remove hot pan from oven
and pour batter into wells, filling about 2/3 full. Bake for about 30
minutes or until lightly brown on top.

MRS. LOYD'S
MEXICAN CORNBREAD
Virginia Loyd

1 cup white self-rising cornmeal
1/4 cup flour
2 eggs
3/4 cup milk
3/4 cup grated Cheddar cheese
1/3 cup cooking oil
1 can (8 oz.) cream-style corn
1/2 Bell pepper, diced
2 small hot peppers, finely chopped
1 medium onion, finely chopped
1/2 teaspoon salt
1/2 teaspoon baking powder

Preheat oven to 400° F. Grease skillet or spray with cooking spray. Mix all ingredients together and bake on bottom rack for 40-45 minutes or until brown.

MEXICAN CORNBREAD
FOR A CROWD
Linda Morris

 2 Lodge
10 1/4 In. Skillets

4 tablespoons cooking oil, divided
3 cups white self-rising cornmeal
1/2 cup finely chopped onion
1/4 cup finely chopped Bell pepper
2 or 3 Jalapeno peppers, chopped
1 2/3 cups grated Cheddar cheese
1 can (15 oz.) cream-style corn
1/2 cup cooking oil
3/4 cup buttermilk
1 cup sour cream
3 eggs beaten
1 1/2 cups plain flour
2 tablespoons sugar
1/2 cup diced pimentos

Put 2 tablespoons oil in each skillet and place in oven while preheating to 400° F. Mix together cornmeal, flour, and sugar. Then add onion, Bell pepper, pimento, Jalapeno peppers. Stir carefully. Add cheese, corn, cooking oil, buttermilk, sour cream, and eggs. Mix well. Divide into hot skillets. Bake for 30-40 minutes or until done.

Variation: Grease a cast iron fluted cake pan, add batter and bake in 400° F oven for about 1 hour, or until done. Let cool a few minutes before inverting cake pan to remove cornbread.

SCALDED CORN CAKES

Wayne LeRoy

 Lodge
10 1/4 In. Skillet

1 teaspoon salt
1 pint boiling water
1 1/4 cups white cornmeal
Vegetable oil or bacon drippings to fill skillet 1 in. deep

Add salt to boiling water; gradually sift in the meal. Cool in refrigerator for 20 minutes. Shape into balls to make patties about two inches across. Fry in 1 inch of fat in skillet until golden brown, about 5 minutes. Turn once. Drain and serve hot.

Wayne loves to cook these when he and his family are at their Battle Creek camp near Monteagle, Tennessee.

SMOKED SAUSAGE AND HOT WATER CORN CAKES

Ibbie Bennett

 Lodge 3 Qt.
Deep Skillet

Enough cooking oil to fill skillet 1 1/2 in. deep
1 cup chopped onions
1 cup cubed smoked sausage
1 small jar pimentos, mashed
2 eggs, slightly beaten
3 cups water, boiling
1 1/2 cups white self-rising cornmeal
1 1/2 cups self-rising flour
1 tablespoon sugar

Turn burner on high and wait for oil to be very hot. In large mixing bowl, combine cornmeal, flour, and sugar. Pour boiling water into dry mix and stir until sticky. Fold slightly beaten eggs into mixture. Add onions, sausage, and pimentos last and stir well. Use large cooking spoon to drop dough into hot cooking oil. Turn cakes 2 or 3 times to brown evenly on both sides. Place on paper towels to drain. Makes 20-25 cakes.

DOC HAVRON'S HUSH PUPPIES

Dr. James B. Havron

Lodge 3 Qt.
Deep Skillet

Lodge
Fry Basket

Corn oil to fill skillet 2 in. deep
2 cups white self-rising cornmeal mix
1 small onion, diced
1/2 red Bell pepper, diced
1/2 green Bell pepper, diced
1 tablespoon sugar
1 tablespoon oil
About 3/4 cup boiling water

In bowl, combine cornmeal mix, oil, and sugar and add enough water until batter will hold together when dropped into frying oil by tablespoons. Then add onions and peppers. Fry until brown in oil about 360° F. Remove from oil and drain on paper towels. Tip: Lodge makes a cornstick pan in the shape of fish and you may use the recipe above for fish shaped hush puppies. Bake in oven at 400° F for about 15-20 minutes.

JODY'S HUSH PUPPIES

Jody McDowell

Lodge 3 Qt.
Deep Skillet

Lodge
Fry Basket

2 cups white self-rising corn meal
3/4 cup milk
1 small onion, finely chopped
1 egg, beaten
Dash of garlic powder
Vegetable oil or shortening to fill skillet 2 in. deep

Combine cornmeal, onion, and garlic powder. Add milk and egg. Mix well. Carefully drop with tablespoon into deep 370° F oil. Never leave oil unattended and protect yourself against splattering. Only cook a few at a time, turning once. Fry until golden brown, about 3-5 minutes. Remove from oil and drain on plate covered with paper towels. Yields about 2 dozen. Tip: If using regular corn meal, add 2 teaspoons baking powder and 1/2 teaspoon salt per cup of meal.

VIRGINIA'S FAVORITE HUSH PUPPIES

Virginia Loyd

Lodge 3 Qt.
Deep Skillet

Lodge
Fry Basket

1 egg
3/4 cup beer
1 cup white self-rising cornmeal
2 1/2 cups self-rising flour
3/4 cup milk
1/2 cup Cheddar cheese, coarsely grated
1 1/2 cups diced onion
1 teaspoon salt
1 teaspoon pepper
1 teaspoon baking powder
3 tablespoons sugar
Vegetable oil to fill skillet 2 in. deep

Mix all ingredients except oil. Chill. Make sure vegetable oil in deep fry skillet is 350° F, using thermometer. Drop in batter with a teaspoon. Remove when golden brown. Drain on paper towels and serve while hot.

Eggs &
Cheese

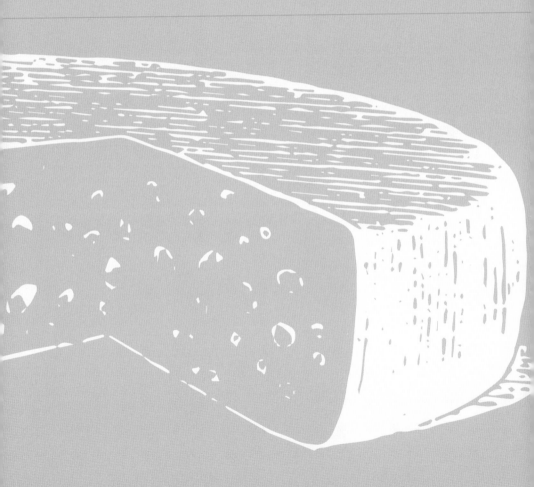

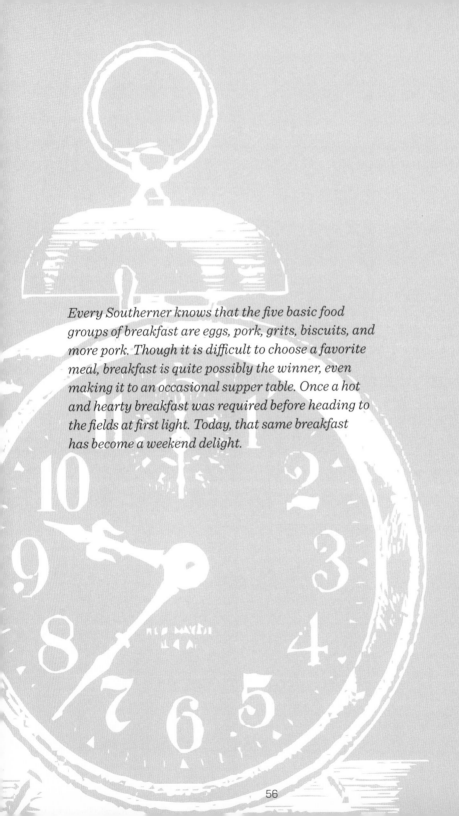

Every Southerner knows that the five basic food groups of breakfast are eggs, pork, grits, biscuits, and more pork. Though it is difficult to choose a favorite meal, breakfast is quite possibly the winner, even making it to an occasional supper table. Once a hot and hearty breakfast was required before heading to the fields at first light. Today, that same breakfast has become a weekend delight.

BOB'S SLOW EGGS

Robert Finch "Bob" Kellermann
CEO Lodge

The size of the skillet depends on the number of eggs being cooked. 1 dozen eggs will fit a 10 1/4 inch skillet. It's important to cook on low heat, and it takes time (typically 40 minutes to cook 18 eggs.) If you're cooking at least a dozen eggs, it's a good idea to start the process before frying your bacon or even preheating the oven for biscuits. Otherwise, you'll be waiting on the eggs to finish when everything else is ready.

> Eggs
> Salt and pepper
> Sharp Cheddar cheese, shredded (about 1 cup per dozen eggs)
> Worcestershire sauce, 2 dashes per egg
> Tabasco sauce, 1 dash per egg
> Bacon drippings or butter, 2-3 tablespoons for 10 1/4 In. skillet
> Paprika (sprinkled on finished eggs before serving)

Lightly oil bottom of skillet with bacon drippings or melted butter. Crack eggs in skillet but do not burst yolks. Add salt and pepper, cheese, Worcestershire (two dashes per egg), Tabasco (one dash per egg). Cook on low heat. When whites begin to cook, rake bottom of skillet with edge of fork, being careful not to break yolks. Continue this process until yolks begin to cook. Cheese and other ingredients will be folded into softly cooked egg whites. Stir yolks into other ingredients as they begin to solidify, yielding yolk chunks that you wouldn't have otherwise. Remove skillet from heat while eggs are still too soft to serve, as heat from skillet will continue cooking process. When eggs have finished cooking sprinkle generously with paprika and serve from your iron skillet.

Secret: Fresh eggs make a difference. I used to get fresh eggs regularly from Roy and Shirley Thomas, who raised chickens on their farm on South Pittsburg Mountain. Shirley is Vice President of Administration for Lodge. Bob cooks the family breakfast on Sundays, continuing the tradition of his father. Francis Kellermann cooked pancakes every Sunday morning. Bob says, "When my children were small, we made 'rainbow' pancakes. The children took red, blue or green food coloring and swirled it into the pancake batter."

CHARLIE'S SCRAMBLED EGGS

Charlie Pickens

Lodge
10 1/4 In. Skillet

6 eggs, beaten
1 can (14 oz.) cream-style corn
1/2 pound bacon, cooked and crumbled
2 tablespoons butter or canola oil
1/4 cup chopped onion
3 tablespoons chopped Bell pepper

Beat eggs. Mix in the corn and bacon with eggs. Melt butter or oil in skillet over medium heat. Add egg mixture and cook. Add onion and pepper just before eggs are completely set. Variation: After frying bacon, sauté onion and pepper in same skillet. Add cooked onion and pepper into egg mixture before they are cooked.

"My dad drives to Lodge Factory Store from Birmingham, Alabama 2 or 3 times a year to buy skillet sets as gifts for family and friends."

FRENCH TOAST
AND FRIED TOMATOES

Barbara Gonce Clepper

Lodge 12 In.
Square Griddle

Lodge
10 1/4 In. Skillet

4 eggs
1/4 cup milk
1/4 teaspoon salt
1/8 teaspoon pepper
4 slices of bread
1/4 cup butter
3 medium sliced tomatoes

In a large glass dish beat together eggs, milk, salt, and pepper. Add bread and let soak 5 minutes on each side, or until egg mixture is absorbed. On a greased 12 Inch griddle, brown soaked bread over medium-low heat. In a separate skillet on medium, heat the butter, add tomatoes and fry on each side 3 minutes. Serve on top of hot French toast. Serves 4.

EGG CASSEROLE FOR A CROWD

2 Lodge
12 In. Skillets

Coughlin Haverty Cooper
from the files of her mother,
Mary Sue Gentry Haverty

1 pound bacon, fried crisp and crumbled
1/2 pound dried beef, chopped
2 cans (6 oz.) sliced mushrooms, drained
1/2 cup (1 stick) butter, divided
1/2 cup flour
1 quart milk
Black pepper to taste
16 eggs
1 cup evaporated milk
1/2 teaspoon salt or to taste

Preheat oven to 275° F. In a bowl, combine bacon, dried beef and half of the mushrooms. In skillet, melt 1/4 cup (1/2 stick) butter. Stir in flour until bubbling and add milk and pepper. Cook and stir over medium-low or medium heat until cream sauce has formed. Remove from heat and add bacon mixture to sauce and set aside. In bowl, mix eggs, evaporated milk, and salt. Melt remaining butter in another skillet. Add egg mixture and scramble over medium heat. Apply cooking spray or butter to a large skillet. Alternate layers of bacon mixture and egg mixture, ending with a layer of bacon mixture. Garnish with remaining mushrooms. Cover and bake for 1 hour. Serves 12.

Tip: Casserole can be made the day before and refrigerated. Remove from refrigerator about 1 hour before baking or slightly extend baking time.

"GO BIG ORANGE" GRITS
Barbara Gonce Clepper

 Lodge 10 1/2 In.
Square Skillets

2 cups chicken broth
2 cups water
1 clove garlic, minced (optional)
1 cup quick-cooking (not instant) grits
1 can (16 oz.) pumpkin puree
2 eggs
1 1/2 cups shredded sharp Cheddar cheese
1/4 teaspoon ground nutmeg
1/4 teaspoon cayenne pepper
Salt and pepper to taste

Preheat oven to 350° F. Place chicken broth, water and garlic in medium size saucepan over high heat. Bring to boil and slowly stir in the grits, stirring constantly. Reduce heat to medium-low and simmer, stirring frequently, about 10 minutes until thickened. Mix in pumpkin puree, stirring until thoroughly combined. Beat eggs in separate bowl. Add small amount of hot grits to beaten eggs and then blend all back into grits mixture. Add cheese, stirring until melted. Season grits with nutmeg, cayenne, salt and pepper. Pour grits into a greased skillet. Bake grits about 50 minutes until set and lightly puffed and brown. Serves 8.

CAST IRON MACARONI AND CHEESE
Marian LeRoy Kohl
Nashville, Tennessee

 Lodge 3 Qt. Deep
Covered Skillet

1 package (8 oz.) macaroni, cooked
16 soda crackers, crushed
1 teaspoon salt
1 teaspoon seasoned pepper
1 cup shredded sharp Cheddar cheese
1 cup shredded extra-sharp Cheddar cheese
6 large eggs, beaten
4 cups milk

Preheat oven to 350° F. In greased deep skillet, spread 1/2 of macaroni, crackers, salt, pepper, and cheeses. Repeat. Whisk together eggs and milk and pour over mixture. Bake for 1 hour. Serves 10.

JALAPENO CHEESE GRITS

Barbara Gonce Clepper

Lodge
Combo Cooker

1 container (32 oz.) chicken broth
1 3/4 cups uncooked quick-cooking grits
1/2 cup butter
1 medium onion, chopped
2 Jalapeno peppers, seeded and diced
1 large green pepper, chopped
2 garlic cloves, pressed
2 cups shredded sharp Cheddar cheese
2 cups shredded Monterey Jack cheese
5 large eggs, beaten
1/4 teaspoon salt

Preheat oven to 350° F. In large saucepan, bring broth to a boil and stir in grits. Reduce heat and simmer for 5 minutes. Stirring often. Cover. Melt butter in deep skillet or Combo Cooker. Add onions, peppers, and pressed garlic cloves, and sauté 5 minutes or until tender. Stir in grits and remaining ingredients. Cover and bake for 45 minutes or until set. Serves 8-10.

RICH MACARONI AND CHEESE

Bertha Russell Gonce

Lodge 3 Qt. Deep
Covered Skillet

1 package (16 oz.) elbow macaroni, cooked
1/2 cup butter
1/2 cup flour
1/2 teaspoon salt
1/2 teaspoon pepper
1/4 teaspoon red pepper
2 cups half-and-half
2 cups milk
20 ounces shredded sharp Cheddar cheese, divided
10 ounces shredded extra-sharp Cheddar cheese

Preheat oven to 350° F. Melt butter in deep skillet over medium-high heat. Gradually stir in flour until smooth. Cook, stirring constantly for 2 minutes. Stir in salt and pepper. Gradually whisk in half-and-half and milk; cook, whisking constantly for 10 minutes. Stir in half of sharp Cheddar cheese. Stir in extra sharp Cheddar cheese until smooth. Remove from heat. Add cooked macaroni and blend well. Sprinkle with the remaining cheese. Bake for 30 minutes. Serves 10.

EASY PIZZA

Carolyn Kellermann Millhiser

Lodge 14 In.
Baking Pan

Lodge
10 1/4 In. Skillet

3 cups Bisquick
3/4 cup water
1 pound ground beef
1/2 cup chopped onion
1/4 teaspoon salt
2 cloves garlic, crushed
1 jar (15 oz.) tomato sauce
1 teaspoon Italian seasoning
1 jar (4 1/2 oz.) sliced mushrooms, drained
1/2 cup chopped green pepper
2 cups shredded Mozzarella cheese

Preheat oven to 425° F. Lightly grease baking pan. Combine baking mix and water until soft dough forms. Gently smooth dough into a ball on floured surface. Knead about 20 times. Pat dough onto baking pan with floured hands, forming rim. Cook and stir ground beef, onion, salt, and garlic until beef is brown; drain. Mix tomato sauce and Italian seasoning; spread evenly over dough. Spoon beef mixture evenly over sauce. Top with mushrooms, green pepper, and cheese. Bake about 20 minutes or until crust is golden brown. Serves 6-8.

MRS. REED'S PIZZA SAUCE

Sarah Reed, owner of the former
Mrs. Reed's Home Bake Shop

1 can (15 oz.) tomato sauce
1 teaspoon onion powder
1 teaspoon garlic powder
1/2 teaspoon Italian seasoning
1 tablespoon Worcestershire sauce
Optional toppings: onions, mushrooms, Bell pepper, pepperoni
2 cups shredded Cheddar cheese and/or Mozzarella cheese

Combine tomato sauce, onion powder, garlic powder, Italian seasoning, and Worcestershire sauce and spread on dough. Top with sliced onion, mushrooms, Bell pepper, and pepperoni. Sprinkle cheeses on top. Bake at 450° F for 15 minutes, per your dough recipe. Enough sauce and toppings for two pizzas.

Whenever anyone would ask Sarah Reed if she ever got tired of baking, she would reply, "I get tired, but never of baking."

LODGE'S PIZZA DOUGH

Chef John Folse
Gonzales, Louisana

Lodge 14 In.
Baking Pan

3 cups bread flour, divided
1 package (1/4 oz.) dry yeast
1 teaspoon salt
1 1/2 teaspoon honey
1 1/4 cups lukewarm water
1 tablespoon olive oil

In a large mixing bowl, mix 1/2 cup of the flour with yeast and salt. Dissolve honey in lukewarm water and add to the mixture. Add olive oil. Mix for three minutes either in the bowl of a mixer or with a wooden spoon. Mix in the remaining flour. (Dough should be slightly sticky.) Knead dough on a floured surface until smooth, about 5 minutes. Place dough in a lightly oiled bowl and cover with plastic wrap. Let rise for 10 minutes in a warm place. Punch dough down and divide in half. Allow the dough to rise 10 additional minutes. Punch down and spread one half by hand or roller onto pan. Preheat oven to 450° F. Top pizza dough with toppings of choice and bake for 12-15 minutes until crust is golden brown. Cool 2-3 minutes before cutting and serving. Dough makes two 13 inch pies.

Tip: Punching down the dough with your fist lets the trapped gasses escape.

Poultry & Dressing

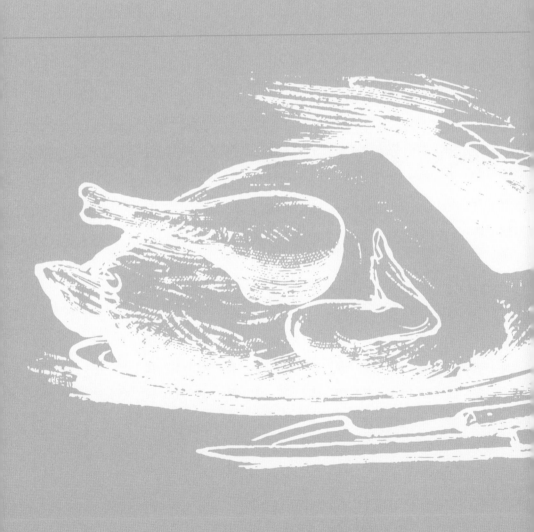

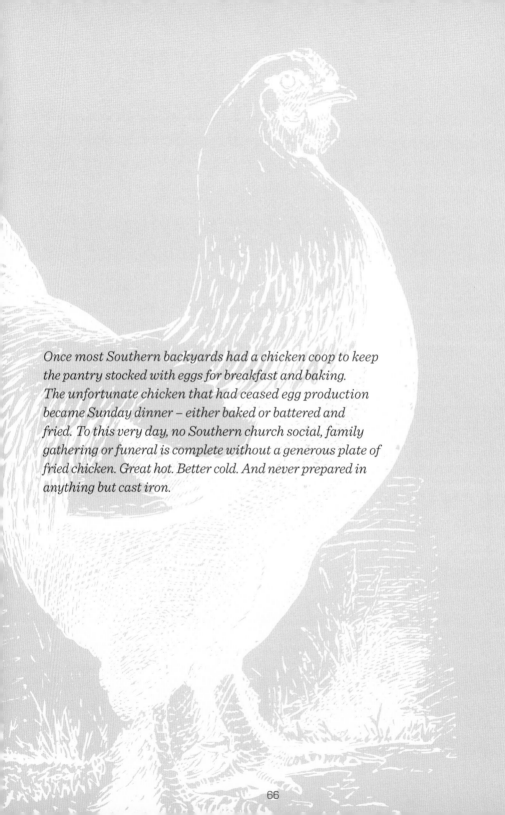

Once most Southern backyards had a chicken coop to keep
the pantry stocked with eggs for breakfast and baking.
The unfortunate chicken that had ceased egg production
became Sunday dinner – either baked or battered and
fried. To this very day, no Southern church social, family
gathering or funeral is complete without a generous plate of
fried chicken. Great hot. Better cold. And never prepared in
anything but cast iron.

BEER CAN CHICKEN
Wade

 Lodge Barbecue
Grill/Grate

4 or 5 pound roasting chicken
1 can (12 oz.) beer
3 tablespoons your favorite dry rub, divided
Canola oil

Start the charcoal grill outside. When it is hot, put the barbecue grill/grate over the rack to give a better balance to the chicken. Remove neck and giblets (to save for fish bait). Rinse chicken inside and out well. Pat dry with paper towels. Coat chicken lightly with oil and season with 2 tablespoons of the dry rub. Set aside. Open beer can, take out about 1/4 cup of beer and make an extra hole in the top of the can with a can opener. Sprinkle the remaining tablespoon of the dry rub inside the beer can. Put the beer can in the center of the grate and set the chicken over the top of the can. The chicken will be sitting on the grate, with the can inside. Close the lid of the grill. Cook chicken for about 1 1/2 hours until the internal temperature is 180° F in the thigh. Remove from the grill, being very careful not to spill the hot contents of the beer can. Let the chicken rest for 10 minutes before carving. Serves about 4.

MOTHER'S FAVORITE FRIED CHICKEN
Billie Cline Hill
A Lodge employee for 59 years

 Lodge 3 Qt. Deep
Covered Skillet

1 cut up frying chicken
1 cup flour
3 teaspoons salt
1 teaspoon pepper

2 eggs
1/4 cup milk
2 cups Crisco

Combine flour, salt, and pepper in a bowl, large enough to hold largest piece of chicken. Put Crisco in deep skillet on medium heat. While oil is getting hot, beat together eggs and milk in a bowl large enough to hold the largest piece of chicken. Dip chicken pieces in egg mixture, and then dredge in flour mixture, then back in egg mixture a second time and back into flour mixture a second time. Then fry slowly until golden brown. You may have to reduce heat as chicken cooks. If the chicken is large or has extra pieces, you may have to mix up more of both wet and dry ingredients.

BAKED CHICKEN AND DRESSING

Carolyn Kellermann Millhiser

Lodge 5 Qt
Dutch Oven

Lodge
Trivet/Meat Rack

3-4 pound roasting chicken or fryer
Option: dressing of choice
Salt and pepper

Use a small whole fryer (about 3 pounds), as it is not as fatty as an older hen. Remove neck and giblets. Soak chicken in a pan of cold salted water about 30 minutes. Remove and rinse chicken inside and out. Salt and pepper cavity. Preheat oven to 350° F. Place chicken on the trivet in Dutch oven. Add 1 cup of water to the Dutch oven. Cover. Bake at 350° F for about 2 1/2 hours. Chicken cooks along happily and makes the house smell good. If you prefer, you can decrease the time to 2 hours by increasing the temperature to 375° F. You and your oven will work out the time and degrees that work for you. Remove chicken and let rest for 20 minutes before serving. Serves 3-4. If baking with dressing in cavity, stuff cavity with dressing before placing on trivet in Dutch oven. Bake at 350° F for 3 hours. Bake leftover dressing covered for 30 minutes before serving.

During World War II, Dick and Lynda Kellermann turned their backyard into a Victory Garden and a small chicken yard. Dick would tend his garden after a day's work at Lodge. The hen that stopped laying eggs became Sunday dinner.

CHICKEN ROSEMARY

Robert Gerlaugh

Lodge 5 Qt
Dutch Oven

6 slices raw bacon
3 pounds chicken pieces
4-6 potatoes, quartered
1 cup sliced green peppers
1 cup sliced mushrooms
2 cups sliced onions

1/2 teaspoon crushed rosemary
1 bay leaf
Salt and pepper to taste
1 large tomato, sliced
1 cup white wine

Preheat oven to 375° F. Layer ingredients in serving pot in order given. Cover. Bake 1 1/2 hours until done. Spoon wine sauce over all and dig in.

JERRY'S DEEP-FRIED CHICKEN

Jerry Clepper

5 pounds chicken pieces
2 or 3 cups buttermilk
2 eggs, beaten
1 pound flour in a clean paper grocery bag
Salt, pepper, and paprika to taste
1 gallon peanut or canola oil

Soak chicken an hour or so in the buttermilk in the refrigerator. Use the fish fry pan and set on propane cooker. This is great for outdoor cooking and you won't have the mess in the house. Fill the pan 2/3 full with peanut oil and start to heat. Have another paper grocery bag lined with several paper towels and a slotted spoon when you start to fry. As oil is heating (never leave oil unattended), drain buttermilk off chicken. Lay it out on wax paper and salt, pepper, and paprika both sides of chicken. Dip chicken pieces in egg, then put a few pieces at a time in the paper bag full of flour and shake to coat well. Use deep fry thermometer to make sure the oil is 350° F. Carefully place dredged chicken in hot oil, one piece at a time to avoid splattering hot oil. Be careful not to overload the pan so that the oil will maintain its temperature. Cook until chicken is golden brown on both sides. Take one piece out to test the inside. Chicken with bones takes longer to cook. If done, remove pieces from oil and place in grocery bag lined with paper towels to drain and keep warm.

Suggestion: Serve with okra, squash, and/or green tomato slices that have been dipped in egg or buttermilk and dredged in flour. Add them to the oil when chicken is done. They only take a minute or so. French fries are also good as a side dish. It is best to put vegetables in a deep fry basket in order to retrieve them easily.

Tip: If you don't have a deep fry thermometer, put a French fry in the oil and when it floats, the oil is ready for the chicken.

In the 1950s, Lodge wanted to make a large cookware piece for frying lots of fish and chicken. One day Leslie Kellermann (who later became president of Lodge) went home and noticed his son's tricycle with a built-in wagon on the back. The next day he took the tricycle to the foundry, and the wagon became the pattern for the Fish Pan which, unfortunately, is not sold today.

69

JERE'S FRIED CHICKEN

Jere R. Brown
Past Co-Chairman of South Pittsburg
Historic Preservation Society

Lodge 5 Qt. Deep
Covered Skillet

Lodge
Fry Basket

2 chickens (3 lb. each) cut into 12 pieces each
1 cup buttermilk
3 cups flour
3 tablespoons paprika
2 teaspoons salt
Black pepper to taste, freshly ground

Sprinkle chicken with milk and let stand at room temperature while combining flour and seasonings in a wide mouth bowl. Dredge chicken in flour and pat on all flour that will stick. Let stand twenty minutes and re-flour. Heat oil, 2 inches deep in iron skillet, to 375° F (using a deep fry thermometer). Add as many pieces of chicken that will fit in one layer. Brown one side of chicken, turn; reduce heat to medium-low. Cover. While covered, turn once. Cook dark meat for 12 minutes, white meat for 6-8 minutes. Remove cover and cook chicken on high heat for 3-5 minutes to re-crisp. Drain on paper towels.

SESAME OVEN-FRIED CHICKEN

Martha Elizabeth "Libby" Austin

Lodge
12 In. Skillet

3 pounds chicken pieces
1/2 cup butter
1 egg, beaten
1/2 cup evaporated milk
1 cup flour
2 teaspoons salt
1 teaspoon pepper
3 teaspoons paprika
1/4 teaspoon baking powder
3 tablespoons sesame seeds

Preheat oven to 400° F. Put butter in skillet and melt in oven. Mix milk and egg in shallow bowl. Mix dry ingredients in another bowl. Coat chicken pieces with milk mixture, then dip into dry mixture. Place in pan, skin side down. Bake uncovered for 25 minutes. Turn chicken pieces over and bake another 25 minutes.

YOUNGIE'S FRIED CHICKEN AND CREAM GRAVY

Youngie Plaster

 Lodge 5 Qt. Deep
Covered Skillet

3 pounds chicken pieces
1 can (13 oz.) evaporated milk
1 tablespoon Worcestershire sauce
3/4 cup flour
3/4 cup plain cornmeal
1 teaspoon salt or to taste
1/2 teaspoon pepper or to taste
Vegetable oil to fill deep skillet 1/2 in. deep

Gravy
1 tablespoon butter
2 tablespoons flour
1/2 cup milk
Salt and pepper to taste

Combine evaporated milk and Worcestershire sauce and mix well. Place chicken in a shallow dish and pour milk mixture over top. Cover and refrigerate 3 hours or overnight. Combine flour, cornmeal, salt, and pepper and mix well. Heat 1/2 inch of oil in deep skillet to 325° F. Meanwhile, drain chicken and dredge chicken pieces in flour and meal mixture. Let stand 5 minutes. Place chicken in hot oil and fry for 30-35 minutes, turning once. Drain chicken on paper towels.

To make cream gravy, reserve 1 1/2 tablespoons of the drippings left in the skillet after frying chicken. Add butter to drippings and melt over low heat. Add flour, stirring until smooth. Cook 1 minute, stirring constantly. Gradually add milk and cook over medium heat, stirring constantly to keep from lumping. Stir in salt and pepper to taste and cook until thick and bubbly.

GRILLED CHICKEN WITH CITRUS SALSA

Ann and Wayne Gray

 Lodge 10 1/4 In. Grill Pan

2 Jalapeno peppers, 1 sliced, 1 minced
1/4 cup plus 1 tablespoon fresh lime juice
1/4 cup plus 1 tablespoon olive oil
4 boneless, skinless chicken breast halves
Salt and pepper to taste
1 naval orange, peeled, sectioned, and cut into 1/4 in. pieces
1 small grapefruit, peeled, sectioned, and cut into 1/4 in. pieces
4 green onions, thinly sliced
10 red cherry tomatoes, seeded and diced
Zest of 1/2 orange
Zest of 1/2 lime
4 handfuls mixed greens

In a shallow bowl, combine Jalapeno slices with 1/4 cup each of the lime juice and olive oil. Rub chicken with salt and pepper and add to the Jalapeno marinade. Marinate in the refrigerator for at least 30 minutes. In a medium size bowl, combine orange, grapefruit, green onions, tomatoes, remaining tablespoon each of lime juice and olive oil, zests, salt, pepper, and minced Jalapeno. Set aside. Remove chicken from marinade. Cook in greased, hot grill pan for 5 minutes on each side, or until cooked through. Remove and let stand for 5 minutes. Divide greens among four plates. Slice chicken and arrange it on top of greens. Spoon salsa over each salad and serve immediately.

JERE BROWN'S STIR FRY CHICKEN

Jere R. Brown

4 tablespoons oil
2 tablespoons Hoisen sauce
Handful of cashew nuts
Hot cooked rice for 4

Chicken Mixture

1 pound boneless, skinless chicken breasts
1 egg white
1 tablespoon cornstarch
2 scallions, chopped
1 teaspoon freshly grated ginger root
2 garlic cloves, minced

Vegetables

1 onion, sliced
1/2 large red pepper, chopped
1/2 large green pepper, chopped
8-10 mushrooms, chunked

Sauce

1/2 cup chicken broth
3 tablespoons soy sauce
2 teaspoons sugar
2 teaspoons dry sherry
1/4 teaspoon salt
1 tablespoon cornstarch

Cut chicken into 1/2 inch pieces. Heat 2 tablespoons oil in wok until hot. Mix chicken mixture in a bowl. Add chicken mixture to hot wok and stir to separate pieces. Cook until mixture turns white. Take chicken out of wok and set aside. Mix sauce in a separate bowl. Add more oil to wok and stir fry vegetables until crisp tender. Return chicken to wok and warm up. Pour sauce into wok and stir until thickened. Add Hoisen sauce and a handful of cashews. Serve over hot rice. Serves 4.

Like many good cooks, Jere Brown does not use recipes so he had to measure the ingredients as he cooked in order to write down the proper amount of ingredients for each recipe he contributed to the cookbook.

CHICKEN A LA KING

Jeanne Mynatt Scholze
Lodge Marketing Director

12 individual pastry shells, baked
2 tablespoons butter
1 cup sliced mushrooms
1/2 cup chopped Bell pepper (about 1/2 Bell pepper)
6 tablespoons butter
6 tablespoons flour
3 cups milk
2 teaspoons salt
4 cups chopped cooked chicken or turkey
4 tablespoons chopped pimento
2 egg yolks, slightly beaten
1/2 cup half and half cream

In skillet, sauté green pepper and mushrooms in butter. Set aside. In Dutch oven, melt butter over medium heat until bubbly. Stir in flour until smooth. Add milk and salt. Cook, stirring constantly until sauce is slightly thick. Remove from heat and add chicken and pimento. Mixture should then be cool enough to add egg yolks without the risk of them starting to cook. Mix well. Return to burner and add mushrooms, Bell pepper and half and half. Heat on low until hot. Serve in individual pastry shells that can be purchased in the frozen food section. Serves 12.

Tips: If using regular pastry shells, and not puff pastry, the shells can be baked a day or two in advance. Cool, put in plastic storage bags, and leave at room temperature. This is especially handy if using this recipe to serve 50-100 people or more.

If freezing, omit the half and half and add it when reheating to serve. For a crowd, make several double recipes as much as a month ahead of event and freeze.

"This recipe came from a dear neighbor who was a home economist by trade over 50 years ago. It remains a fabulous recipe to serve on gala occasions. It served 350 people on the occasion of my parents Fiftieth Wedding Anniversary. In 2001, it was served at the 125th Anniversary of Christ Church Episcopal, South Pittsburg, Tennessee."

CHICKEN AND PORTOBELLO MUSHROOMS
Howard Skyler

 Lodge 10 1/2 In.
Square Skillets

4 skinless, boneless chicken breast halves
1 medium onion, diced
2 ribs celery, diced
1/2 can (15 oz.) diced tomatoes
1/4 medium Bell pepper, diced
1 can cream of chicken soup
1/3 cup sour cream
1/3 cup sherry or cooking sherry
1 large Portobello mushroom cut into bite size pieces
Hot rice or noodles

Preheat oven to 325° F. Cut chicken into bite-size pieces.
Combine all ingredients except rice or noodles. Place mixture
in lightly oiled skillet. Bake about 45 minutes. Serve with rice or
noodles. Serves 4.

MARY JANE'S HOT CHICKEN SALAD
Mary Jane Brown

 Lodge 10 1/2 In.
Square Skillets

2 cups cooked chicken, cut into chunks
2 cups chopped celery
3 tablespoons minced onion
3 tablespoons lemon juice
1/2 teaspoon salt
1/2 teaspoon black pepper
1/2 cup chopped pecans
3/4 cup mayonnaise
1 can (4 oz.) sliced mushrooms
1 can cream of mushroom soup
Potato chips for garnish

Preheat oven to 300° F. Combine all ingredients except soup
and chips. Mix well. Place in lightly greased skillet. Spread soup
over mixture. Do not stir. Top with crushed potato chips. Bake
for 30 minutes. Serves 6 to 8. Serve with cranberry sauce or
congealed salad.

CURRIED CHICKEN OR TURKEY

Sarah Kirkwood "Pat" Lodge
mother of Henry Lodge, President of Lodge

Lodge 5 Qt.
Dutch Oven

6 cups chicken or turkey, cooked and cut up
2 cups chicken broth
10 tablespoons butter
1 cup onion, minced
12 tablespoons flour (scant 2/3 cup)
2 tablespoons curry powder mixed with flour
2 teaspoons salt
3 teaspoons sugar
4 cups milk
Hot rice for 12
Condiments
(Use Lodge 1/2 Pint Serving Kettles for Condiments)
Coconut
Roasted peanuts, chopped
Crisp bacon, chopped
Chutney

Melt the butter in the Dutch oven. Add onion and stir until onion is golden in color. Stir in the flour and make a paste. Gradually add the broth while stirring constantly. Add milk, salt, and sugar. Add chicken. Serve over rice with at least 4 condiments. Serves 12. This recipe can be used for leftover beef or lamb.

Pat remembers the leftover main dish from Sunday's dinner reappearing midweek as a curried dish at her grandmother's farm, Roamer's Roost, in Southern Alabama.

MARY FLORENCE PADGETT SMITH'S CHICKEN LOAF

Roberta Padgett Robinson

 2 Lodge Loaf Pans

5 pound hen or 4 cups cooked chicken
1/3 cup raw rice or 1 cup cooked rice
3 cups chicken broth
2 cups fresh bread crumbs
1 1/2 teaspoons salt
1 small jar pimentos, diced and drained
1 tablespoon onion, minced
5 or 6 eggs, beaten

Sauce
1 cup sour cream
1 can cream of mushroom soup

In a Dutch oven simmer the hen in salted water until tender. The trivet will prevent scorching when used in the bottom of the Dutch oven. Cook 2 1/2 to 3 hours. Pull meat off bone after it has cooled a short time and chop into fine pieces. Cook rice in 1 cup of the chicken broth. Preheat oven to 350° F. Grease and line loaf pans with waxed paper. This is very important to keep mixture from sticking to bottom of pan. Put chopped chicken, cooked rice, and bread crumbs in a large bowl. Add salt, pimentos, 2 cups broth, onion, and eggs to the mixture and blend well. Pour into the loaf pans and bake for one hour. This will appear quite moist but sets up as it bakes and unmolds easily. Serve with sauce made from sour cream heated slowly with cream of mushroom soup.

MISS MARY'S CHICKEN SALAD

Mary McRae Griffith

2 cups cooked and diced skinless chicken
1 cup diced celery
1/2 cup diced blanched almonds
Mayonnaise to hold salad together

French Dressing
1 tablespoon sugar
1 teaspoon salt
9 tablespoons Wesson oil
1 teaspoon dry mustard
3 tablespoons vinegar
Juice of a lemon
Dash of red pepper or paprika

Place diced chicken in a large bowl. Pour the French dressing over chicken and let it stand covered and refrigerated overnight or at least 3 to 4 hours. Then add celery and nuts to the chicken and mix with a small amount of mayonnaise. Careful not too much mayonnaise.

Suggestion: Pretty and good if served on bed of lettuce, as stuffing for a tomato or as filling for half an avocado. Don't peel avocado until very last and squeeze lemon over it to keep from discoloring.

Tip: For a party, double the recipe-takes one large hen or chicken.

Mary McRae was born in South Pittsburg. In 1888 Owen Russell Beene hired her father, Angus McRae, to construct a small sandstone Gothic revival church for the Primitive Baptists of South Pittsburg. Her son, Hugh A. Griffith, Jr. and George Harvey Kellermann, Joseph Lodge's grandson, often checked what menus the mothers had planned before deciding where the two fast friends would eat.

DOC HAVRON'S DUCK
Doctor James Blackman "Jimmy" Havron

Lodge
10 1/4 In. Skillet

4-6 wild duck breasts
1 can evaporated milk
1 egg, beaten
1/4 cup soy sauce
1 tablespoon seasoning salt
1 tablespoon Worcestershire sauce
2 drops Tabasco sauce
1 cup flour
1/2-3/4 cup chopped green onions
Salt and pepper to taste
Canola oil to fill skillet about 1/2 in. deep

Combine milk, egg, soy, seasoning salt, Worcestershire sauce, and Tabasco sauce into a glass bowl large enough to hold duck breasts. Cut duck breasts into finger-sized strips and place in bowl with marinade. Cover and refrigerate overnight. When ready to fry, chop green onion and set aside. Fill skillet to about 1/2 inch deep with canola oil and turn heat to medium. While oil is heating, place duck strips on wax paper and discard marinade. Salt and pepper duck to taste, then dredge in flour. Fry on medium heat, with chopped green onions, until duck is tender and done.

CORNBREAD, SAUSAGE, AND CRANBERRY DRESSING

Lodge
13 1/4 In. Skillet

Barbara Gonce Clepper

3 cups day old cornbread
  crumbled
1/2 pound pork sausage
3 tablespoons butter
1 large onion, chopped
2 stalks celery, diced
1 carrot, chopped

1 cup chopped fresh
  cranberries
1 1/2 tablespoons maple syrup
Zest of 1 orange
1 1/2 tablespoons chopped
  rosemary
Salt and pepper to taste

Make cornbread. Cool. Crumble and refrigerate overnight in covered bowl. When ready to make dressing, set the oven at 350° F to preheat. Brown sausage in skillet over medium-high heat. Use wooden spoon to crumble sausage and cook until brown and beginning to crisp; about 10-15 minutes. Remove from skillet with slotted spoon and place in a large mixing bowl. Add butter to sausage drippings remaining in pan and let melt over medium heat. Stir in onion, celery, and carrot. Sauté until vegetables are soft, about 15 minutes. Combine vegetables with sausage. Stir in crumbled cornbread. Mix chopped cranberries with maple syrup. Add to dressing mixture. Mix orange zest and rosemary into dressing and season to taste with salt and pepper. Dressing can be used to stuff turkey, but I think it is better and safer placed in a greased skillet and baked for about 1 hour or until golden brown.

DONNY'S DRESSING

2 Lodge 10 1/2 In.
Square Skillets

Donny Walker

1 stick butter, melted
1/2 cup chopped onion
3/4 cup chopped celery
3 packages (8 oz.) plain stuffing mix
1 1/2 cups chopped pecans
1 large can sliced mushrooms
6 hard boiled eggs, chopped
6 cans chicken broth

Preheat oven to 350° F. In the skillet, sauté onion and celery in a little of the butter. Place the stuffing mix in a large mixing bowl and add pecans, mushrooms, sautéed onion and celery, eggs, broth, and butter. Add additional broth if mixture is not moist enough. Mixture will fill two 12 inch skillets. Bake for 30-45 minutes. Serves 12-16.

MILLIE'S CORNBREAD DRESSING

Millie McDonald

Lodge 7 Qt.
Dutch Oven

Cornbread (using your own recipe)
1/4 box saltine crackers (1 stack), crumbled
1 cup chopped celery
1 teaspoon sage
1/4 teaspoon salt
3 eggs, beaten
1/2 cup butter, melted
6 slices toasted bread, crumbled
1 medium onion, diced
1 teaspoon poultry seasoning
1/8 teaspoon oregano
8 cups chicken broth

Best if you can bake cornbread the day before and store it crumbled, in refrigerator until ready to use. Preheat oven to 400° F. Combine and thoroughly mix all ingredients. Add enough chicken broth to make the mixture very moist but not soupy. Pour into greased Dutch oven. Bake for 1 1/2 hours or until brown on top.

MRS. REED'S CORNBREAD DRESSING

Sarah Reed

2 Lodge 10 1/2 In.
Square Skillets

1 skillet of cornbread, using your favorite recipe
8 cups chicken broth, or as much as needed
1/2 cup chopped green onion
1/2 cup shredded carrots
1 tablespoon chopped parsley
1 teaspoon black pepper
1 tablespoon sage
6 hard boiled eggs, chopped

Make cornbread and cool. Store in a tightly covered bowl, in the refrigerator overnight. Preheat oven to 400° F when ready to make dressing. Crumble cornbread in big bowl. Add onions, carrots, parsley, eggs, black pepper, and sage. Stir in enough broth to make a slightly thin mixture. Gently stir in the eggs. Pour into greased hot skillets and bake for 30 minutes or until brown.

SEQUATCHIE SQUASH DRESSING

Betty Mayfield Thomas

Lodge
12 In. Skillet

2 cups prepared cornbread, cooled and crumbled
3 cups sliced squash
1 onion, chopped
1 pound sausage
1 can cream of chicken soup
1/2 cup milk
1 egg, beaten
1 teaspoon salt
1 teaspoon sage
1/4 teaspoon pepper
1 cup shredded Cheddar cheese, divided
2 tablespoons butter

Make a skillet of cornbread or use leftovers to make 2 cups. Cook squash in water and drain when tender. Set aside. Preheat oven to 375° F. Sauté onion and sausage. Drain when brown. Add butter to sausage. In a mixing bowl, combine cornbread crumbs, soup, milk, and egg. Add sausage and butter to cornbread mixture. Mix in salt, sage, pepper, and part of cheese. Pour into skillet, top with remainder of cheese and bake for 50 minutes or until done.

DONNY'S EASY DUMPLINGS

Donny Walker

Lodge 5 Qt.
Dutch Oven

5 cans chicken broth
1 can cream of mushroom soup
1 can cream of celery soup
Cooked, chopped chicken or turkey (Optional)
2 packages (20 oz.) flour tortilla shells

In Dutch oven heat broth and soups until boiling. Add chopped chicken, if desired. Cut the tortillas into 1 inch squares and add to the broth mixture. Simmer a few minutes until tortillas are tender.

Fish &
Seafood

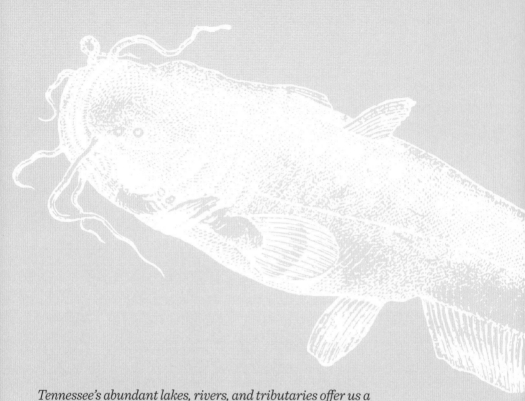

Tennessee's abundant lakes, rivers, and tributaries offer us a meal that costs little more than some line, bait, and a relaxing afternoon on a river bank. Today's seafood market offers a gracious bounty from inland waterways to the oceans of the world. Nevertheless, this is the region of the catfish. Farm-raised, fingered, or filleted, it is served up one way – fried. Whether it's at the campsite at Mud Creek or at the Catfish House on the Tennessee River, it is never without coleslaw and hush puppies.

DEEP-FRIED CATFISH

Jerry Clepper

5 pounds fish fillets, all cut to about the same size
Salt and pepper to taste
Small jar of prepared yellow mustard
3 cups flour
3 cups cornmeal
(Or 6 cups Zatarain's Fish Fry)
1 gallon canola oil

Mount the fish fry pan on a propane burner and cook outdoors. Fill pan 2/3 full with canola oil and start to heat oil to 360° F with assigned guest keeping a watchful eye on it. It is best to use a deep fry thermometer. Combine flour and cornmeal (or Zatarain's Fish Fry) into clean paper grocery bag. Lay fillets out on cookie pans lined with wax paper. Season both sides of fish with salt and pepper. Coat each piece with about 1/2 teaspoon prepared mustard. Drop each fillet into flour and cornmeal mixture and shake bag to coat well. Before you start to fry, have another paper bag lined with several paper towels and a slotted spoon ready at the cooker. Place fillets one at a time into hot oil. Be careful not to overload so that the oil will maintain its temperature. Take up the fish soon after it floats but not until it has become light brown. Place cooked fish fillets in grocery bag lined with paper towels to drain and keep warm. After all the fish is cooked, place French fries and hush puppies into the oil. Serve with coleslaw, tartar sauce, and ketchup.

"A big catch in the Tennessee River calls for a Clepper family gathering. The fish and hush puppies never make it to the table, because they are gobbled up by the cook and the samplers as soon as it gets done."

PAN-FRIED CATFISH
Frances Porter

Lodge
12 In. Skillet

Canola oil to fill skillet 1/4 in. deep
4 catfish fillets (or fish of choice), filleted and fingered
Salt and pepper to taste
Cajun seasoning or lemon pepper to taste
1 cup cornmeal
1 cup flour
1 cup buttermilk

Heat oil in skillet on medium heat until hot. Combine flour and cornmeal in wide-mouth bowl. Lay fish pieces on wax paper and season with salt, pepper, and seasoning of choice. Turn fish over and season on other side. Dip seasoned pieces of fish into buttermilk, and then dredge in cornmeal-flour mixture. Arrange in skillet and brown slowly on both sides. Drain on paper towels. Serve with coleslaw and hush puppies or cornbread.

BAKED CRAPPIE FILLETS
Jim Clepper

Lodge
13 1/4 In. Skillet

6 large crappie fillets
1 large can Durkee's French-fried onion rings, crushed
1 medium bottle ranch dressing

Preheat oven to 375° F. Spray skillet with cooking spray. Dip fillets in dressing, and then coat with crushed onion rings. Place fillets in skillet and bake for 20 minutes.

Crappie is a perch-like sunfish. Pronounced Croppie in Tennessee. Pronounced Crappie elsewhere.

FRIED CRAPPIE

Jim Clepper

Lodge 3 Qt.
Deep Skillet

Lodge
Fry Basket

2 quarts canola oil
12 crappie fillets
2 cups cornmeal
1/4 teaspoon garlic powder, or to taste
1 teaspoon paprika, or to taste
1 teaspoon salt, or to taste
1/2 teaspoon pepper, or to taste
3/4 cup milk

Heat canola oil in skillet until 360° F. Lay fish on wax paper and sprinkle spices on the fish to taste. Dredge fillets in cornmeal, then dip in milk, and back into the cornmeal. Place a few fillets in fry basket and fry until golden brown. Serve with coleslaw and hush puppies.

CUMBERLAND CRAB CAKES

Jody McDowell

Lodge
10 1/4 In. Skillet

1 1/2 pounds crab meat
1 egg, beaten
2 tablespoons mayonnaise
Salt to taste
Freshly ground black pepper to taste
Hot sauce to taste
4 tablespoons salted butter
1 tablespoon olive oil

Combine crab meat, egg, mayonnaise, and seasonings in a bowl and mix. Form into small cakes and place on cookie sheet lined with wax paper and refrigerate for 20 minutes. Heat butter and olive oil in skillet on medium heat. Cook crab cakes until golden brown on both sides (about 4 minutes per side). Serve hot.

Tip: Olive oil helps keep butter from burning.

SALMON BAKE PHINEAS

Phineas Howard Syler

Lodge 10 1/2 In.
Square Skillets

2 1/2 cups rice, cooked
1 can (15 oz.) can salmon, juice and all unless you prefer to
* remove bones*
1 can cream of celery soup
3 cloves garlic, pressed
2 teaspoons dried basil
1 tablespoon lemon juice
1 large egg, beaten
1/3 cup sour cream

Dressing

1/2 cup sour cream
1/2 cup mayonnaise
1/2 large cucumber, peeled and grated

Preheat oven to 350° F. Lightly grease skillet or spray with
cooking spray. Combine ingredients and pour into pan. Bake about
45 minutes, or until center is firm. Combine dressing ingredients in
small bowl. Serve with dressing.

SALMON PATTIES

Frances Porter
Tuscumbia, Alabama

Lodge
10 1/4 In. Skillet

6 tablespoons cooking oil
1 can (15 oz.) salmon
2 eggs, beaten
1/4 cup milk
1/2 teaspoon salt

1/2 teaspoon pepper
1/2 cup cracker crumbs
1 teaspoon lemon juice
1 tablespoon catsup

Drain salmon and remove skin. Combine eggs, milk, then add
salmon. Add seasonings, cracker crumbs, lemon juice, and
catsup. Shape into patties. Heat cooking oil in skillet on medium
heat. Place patties in skillet and brown on both sides, about 10
minutes per side.

Variation: For salmon loaf, bake in lightly greased Lodge loaf pan
at 350° For about 45 minutes or until lightly brown.

SKILLET SALMON

Jeanne Mynatt Scholze

 Lodge
10 1/4 In. Skillet

1 tablespoon butter
1 or 2 tablespoons olive or canola oil
2 serving pieces of fresh salmon fillets
1 fresh lemon
Freshly chopped dill to taste
Kosher salt to taste
2 or 3 tablespoons mayonnaise (can use light)

Melt butter and oil in skillet on top of stove on medium heat. Place salmon fillets on plate, skin side down. Generously squeeze juice of lemon over fillets. Sprinkle with dill and salt over fillets. Spread light coat of mayonnaise over fillets. Place salmon, mayonnaise-side down, into hot skillet. Allow to brown on medium heat before turning. Then cook skin side down for about 4 minutes. Turn the salmon over and peel off the skin. Then squeeze lemon, salt, and dill onto the skin side of the salmon. Turn the salmon back over and brown. If the salmon fillets are thick, it may be necessary to reduce heat to medium-low and cook a few more minutes until cooked through, but take care not to overcook. Remove from skillet and serve immediately.

SEAFOOD AND RICE

Jayne Clepper Halvorson

 Lodge 3 Qt. Deep
Covered Skillet

1/2 cup butter or margarine
1/4 cup chopped Bell pepper
1 large onion, chopped
1/4 cup finely chopped celery
2 cloves garlic, minced
1 pound shrimp, peeled
1 teaspoon salt
1/2 teaspoon black pepper
1/4 teaspoon white pepper
1/2 teaspoon onion powder
1/2 teaspoon hot sauce
1 1/2 tablespoons flour
3/4 cup water
1/2 cup chopped green onions
1/4 cup chopped fresh parsley
Hot cooked rice for 6

Put butter in deep skillet or serving pot and melt over medium heat. Add onion, celery, and Bell pepper. Cook 5 minutes, stirring constantly. Add shrimp, salt, peppers, onion powder, and hot sauce. Cook 5 minutes, then add flour. Cook 2 more minutes, stirring constantly. Add water gradually. Reduce heat to low and cook an additional 20 minutes, stirring occasionally. Mix in green onions, parsley, and cook for 3 minutes. Serve over rice. Serves 6.

SEAFOOD SKILLETS

Jack Ransley
Hendersonville, North Carolina

1 egg, beaten
1/2 cup bread crumbs
Dash Tabasco sauce
1 teaspoon lemon juice
1/2 cup cream
1 tablespoon cooking oil
1/2 cup finely chopped celery
1/2 cup finely chopped onions
4 fish fillets
8 medium shrimp, peeled
8 scallops

Optional Toppings

1/2 cup cracker crumbs
2 teaspoons butter

Mix together first five ingredients and set aside. Preheat oven to 350° F. Heat the oil in one of the skillets and sauté the onions and celery. Divide the onions and celery into the four skillets. Then layer 1 fish fillet, 2 shrimp and 2 scallops into each skillet. Pour the topping mix evenly over each skillet.

Top with cracker crumbs and 1/2 teaspoon butter. Bake for 30 minutes, then brown under broiler for about 5 minutes.

SKILLET SHRIMP

Mrs. Charles H. Young, Sr.
Slidell, Louisiana

 Lodge 3 Qt. Deep
Covered Skillet

1/2 stick butter
1 small bunch green onions with tops, chopped
2 cloves garlic, minced
2 pounds small shrimp, cleaned
Salt to taste
Red pepper to taste
Black pepper to taste
Juice from 1 lemon
1/2 cup chopped fresh parsley
Cooked rice for 6 servings

Melt butter in skillet. Wilt onions and garlic in butter. Add shrimp and season with salt and peppers. Cover skillet with lid and cook on low setting for 5 minutes. Turn shrimp over; add lemon juice and parsley. Cover and cook for 5 minutes more. Serve over rice with hot rolls and salad.

TUNA FISH A LA KING
Mildred Clepper

3 tablespoons butter
1 tablespoon chopped green pepper
3 tablespoons flour
2 cups milk
1 can (12 oz.) flaked tuna, drained
1/2 small can English peas
3 tablespoons sliced stuffed olives
1 teaspoon Worcestershire sauce
Paprika to taste
Salt to taste

In the deep skillet, melt the butter and sauté the green pepper. Don't let the pepper brown. Put the milk and flour into a clean mayonnaise jar with lid and shake until blended. Pour into the melted butter and cook over medium-low heat. Stir until sauce is slightly thick. Add the remaining ingredients and cook on low heat for about 20 minutes until hot. Serve hot on popovers, quick rolls, biscuits, or pastry shells. Serves 6.

Meat

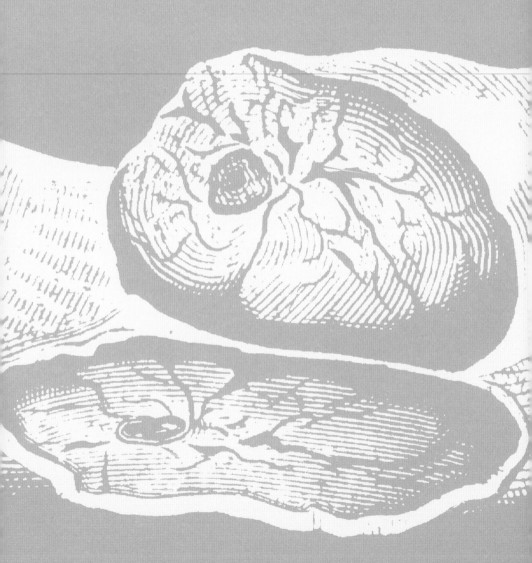

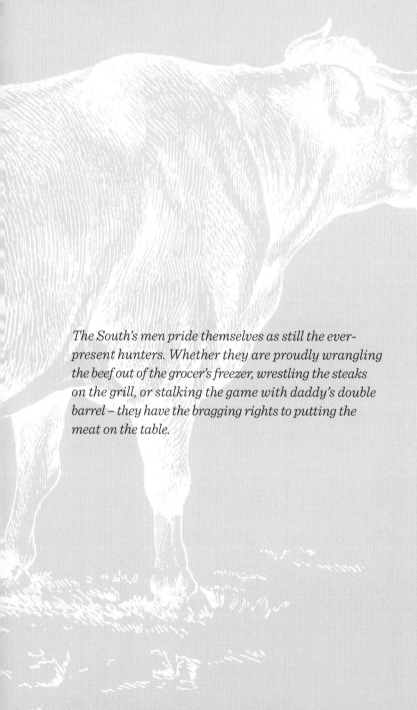

The South's men pride themselves as still the ever-present hunters. Whether they are proudly wrangling the beef out of the grocer's freezer, wrestling the steaks on the grill, or stalking the game with daddy's double barrel – they have the bragging rights to putting the meat on the table.

BARON OF BEEF AU JUS

Norma Ryding Neperud

Lodge 5 Qt.
Dutch Oven

> *1 tablespoon cooking oil*
> *4 pound rump or sirloin tip roast*
> *1 package Lipton's onion soup mix*
> *1 can (15 oz.) chicken broth*
> *1 bay leaf*

Heat oil in Dutch oven on top of stove. Turn heat to medium-high and place roast in Dutch oven and sear until brown on all sides. Add onion soup mix, chicken broth, and bay leaf. Cover and bake in 275° F oven for 4 hours or until done. It will take 6 hours if you start with a frozen roast. Remove the bay leaf and slice the roast. Serve with whipped potatoes and biscuits to take advantage of the delicious gravy. Serves 6.

AUNT MARY'S POT ROAST

Virginia "Ginger" England

Lodge 5 Qt.
Dutch Oven

> *4 or 5 pound chuck roast*
> *1 can beer*
> *1 envelope Good Seasons Italian Dressing*

Put roast in Dutch oven and place on top of stove on high setting to sear on all sides. Then add the beer and Italian Dressing. Set oven to 275° F or 300° F and bake for 3 or 4 hours. Serves 6.

Variation: Add quartered onions, celery strips, carrots, and potatoes for the last hour of cooking.

Cast iron Dutch ovens were the original slow cookers. They are perfect for turning less tender cuts of meat into tender and juicy results, when cooked with liquid.

CHINESE PEPPER STEAK

Gladys Streeter Wooten

Lodge 3 Qt. Deep
Covered Skillet

2 pound boneless chuck steak
2 tablespoons bacon grease or Crisco
1 bunch green onions, sliced
1 1/2 cups sliced celery
2 cloves garlic, minced
Salt and pepper to taste
2 beef bouillon cubes
1 cup hot water
2 large green peppers cut into eighths
2 tablespoons cornstarch
1/4 cup cold water
1 tablespoon soy sauce
Hot cooked rice to serve 4

Trim fat from the beef and cut the beef into thin strips. Heat the bacon grease or shortening in deep skillet and brown meat. Cover and cook over low heat until tender. Add onions, celery, garlic, salt, and pepper. Dissolve bouillon cubes in the hot water and add to the meat. Add the vegetables and cook until they are partially done, but still crisp. Add the green pepper and cook 5 minutes over very low heat. Blend the cornstarch with the cold water and add to the meat. Cook and stir until the gravy is thickened. Add soy sauce and serve over fluffy rice. Serves 4.

CUBED STEAK WITH GRAVY

Doris Marsh Durham

Lodge 3 Qt. Deep
Covered Skillet

6 cubed steaks
Salt and pepper to taste
1 cup flour, sifted onto wax paper
1 stick butter
1/8 cup water

Preheat oven to 250° F. Lay steaks on wax paper and salt and pepper to taste. Dredge steaks in flour. Melt butter in deep skillet on medium-high heat. When butter is hot, add steaks. Reduce heat to medium and let steaks brown on both sides. Place steaks in skillet and add water. Set deep skillet aside with drippings to use in gravy. Cover skillet with the cover from the deep skillet and bake for 1 hour.

Gravy

2 tablespoons flour
Salt and pepper to taste
About 3/4 cup water
1/8 cup cream

While steak is steaming in oven, place deep skillet back on medium heat. Add just enough flour to drippings in skillet to make a paste. Brown slowly until just before burning. Add enough water to make gravy. Salt and pepper to taste. When it starts to thicken, add cream. Heat through. Serve over steak.

TENDER CUBE STEAK WITH MUSHROOM GRAVY

Nancy Ballard

Lodge 5 Qt. Deep
Covered Skillet

4 or 5 cube steaks
Salt and pepper to taste
Garlic salt to taste
Flour for dredging
2 tablespoons olive oil
1 can (4 oz.) sliced mushrooms
1 medium onion, chopped
1 can cream of mushroom soup

Salt and pepper each cube steak. Sprinkle garlic salt on each steak, and then dredge in flour to coat on both sides. Heat olive oil to medium-high heat in deep skillet. Preheat oven to 350° F. Brown steaks on both sides. Put mushrooms and onion into fryer with cube steaks. Add soup and one can of water. Cover the fryer with lid and bake in oven for 1 hour. Serves 4-5. Serve with creamed potatoes or rice to take advantage of the gravy.

Nancy, a hobby painter, was the first to decorate the "skillet" crown awarded to the Champion of the National Cornbread Cook-off sponsored by Lodge Manufacturing and Martha White at the National Cornbread Festival held in South Pittsburg the last weekend in April each year.

ROUND STEAK IN WINE SAUCE

Sarah Kirkwood Lodge

Lodge
12 In. Skillet

3 pound round steak about 1 1/2 in. thick
2 tablespoons butter
1 1/2 cups chopped onion
2 tablespoons prepared mustard
1 teaspoon Worcestershire sauce
1 cup sliced fresh mushrooms
1/2 teaspoon salt
1/4 cup dry red wine
1/2 cup water
1 or 2 tablespoons flour

Heat butter on medium heat in skillet. Turn heat to medium-high and brown steak on all sides. Reduce heat to low. Add all remaining ingredients except flour and combine well. Cover and simmer for 2 hours or until meat is tender. If desired, add more liquid in the percentage of 1 part wine to 2 parts water. Remove meat from skillet and keep warm. Add flour to pan juice, blend well, and simmer 3 minutes. Add more liquid if needed. Serve with meat. Serves 6.

JUNE'S MEAT LOAF

June Chance

Lodge
Loaf Pan

3/4 pound ground beef
1/4 pound pork sausage
1 egg, beaten
1 teaspoon salt
1/4 teaspoon pepper
3/4 cup canned tomatoes
1/2 cup crushed saltines

Preheat oven to 350° F. Mix all ingredients together. Put into loaf pan. Bake 1 hour. Serves 4-5.

BARBECUE BEEF BRISKET

Linda Ellis Cole

 Lodge 5 Qt.
Dutch Oven

4 pound beef brisket
2 tablespoons liquid smoke
1 teaspoon crushed bay leaf
2 tablespoons chili powder
1 1/2 teaspoons pepper
1 1/2 teaspoons salt

Preheat oven to 325° F. Place meat, fat side up, in a Dutch oven. Rub meat completely with liquid smoke. Combine salt, pepper, chili powder, and bay leaves. Sprinkle dry seasoning mixture on top of meat. Cover and bake 4 hours. Remove from oven and scrape seasoning off. Cut meat across the grain in very thin slices. Serve with barbecue sauce.

Barbecue Sauce

2 tablespoons brown sugar
1 bottle (14 oz.) catsup
1/2 cup water
2 tablespoons liquid smoke
Salt and pepper to taste
4 tablespoons Worcestershire sauce
3 teaspoons dry mustard
2 teaspoons celery seed
6 tablespoons butter
1/4 teaspoon red pepper

Combine all ingredients and bring to boil on medium heat. Stir and cook for 10 minutes. Serve with brisket.

STOVE TOP BARBECUE
Betty Mayfield Thomas

 Lodge 3 Qt. Deep Covered Skillet

3 pound chuck, sirloin or rump roast
Salt, pepper, and garlic powder to taste
Cooking oil for browning
1 onion, chopped
1 tablespoon Worcestershire sauce
2 teaspoons Heinz 57 sauce

Rub meat with salt, pepper, and garlic powder. Brown on medium-high heat in a little oil in the deep skillet. Reduce heat to low. Add chopped onion to one side. Add Worcestershire sauce, cover, and cook on very low heat about 3 to 4 hours, or until so tender that the meat pulls apart with a fork. Most of the liquid will cook down. Add Heinz 57 sauce for the barbecue flavor. Stir to mix the onions and Heinz well. Serve on hot buns for a delicious sandwich.

"Go ahead and use your iron skillets on your glass top stoves. Just don't drop them!"

NORMA'S TENNESSEE BEEF SKILLET
Norma Ryding Neperud

 Lodge 3 Qt. Deep Covered Skillet

1 pound ground beef
3/4 cup chopped onion
1 can (15 oz.) tomatoes with liquid, chopped
1 can (15 oz.) kidney beans with liquid
1/2 cup uncooked rice
3 tablespoons chopped green pepper
1 1/2 teaspoons chili powder
1/2 teaspoon garlic salt
1/2 teaspoon salt
1/2 cup water
3/4 cup shredded Cheddar cheese
Corn chips, crushed

Fry ground beef and onion in skillet. Drain. Stir in tomatoes, kidney beans, rice, green pepper, chili powder, garlic salt, salt, and water. Bring to a boil then reduce heat. Simmer, covered for 20 minutes, stirring occasionally. Top with cheese, cover and heat 3 minutes. Serve over corn chips. Serves 4.

STEAK TERIYAKI

Dr. James Blackman Havron
affectionately called "Dr. Jimmy" for
over 50 years by all of South Pittsburg.

Lodge
14 In. Wok

1/3 pound rib-eye steaks per person, special butcher cuts
Suet (butcher trimmings from the steak)
Hot cooked rice for each person

Sauce
1/2 cup soy sauce
1/4 cup sherry
4 tablespoons sugar
2 thin slices fresh ginger

Have butcher cut rib-eye steaks to thickness of thin bacon.
At that time, request the butcher to save the trimmings from
the steak for the suet. Prepare the meat by laying out the strips
and cutting them into pieces that can be rolled into thumb or
"bite-size" pieces. Roll meat and place on platter. Slice the suet
remnants into bite-size pieces. Place all ingredients for the sauce
in a sauce pan and bring to a boil. Heat cast iron wok and have
the sauce at hand with the rolled meat and suet. Line sides with
2-3 pieces of suet, which will drizzle down to the middle and
serve as oil. Dip rolls of meat into the sauce and place into the
hot oil. Cook briefly 2-3 pieces at a time and serve immediately
over rice to each guest.

CLARICE'S SQUASH-HAMBURGER CASSEROLE

Clarice O'Neal Adcock

2 pounds yellow squash, sliced
1 medium onion, chopped
1 pound hamburger meat
3 tablespoons butter
1 egg, beaten

1 teaspoon salt or to taste
1 teaspoon pepper or to taste
5 soda crackers, crumbled
1/2 cup grated cheese

Boil squash and onion in small amount of water until tender. Drain well and mash. Combine squash and onion mixture with butter, egg, salt, pepper, and crackers in mixing bowl. Preheat oven to 350° F. Sauté hamburger meat in skillet. Remove from heat. Combine squash mixture with hamburger meat. Top with cheese. Bake 30 minutes.

BARBARA'S REFRIGERATOR HASH

Barbara Gonce Clepper

Lodge Combo Cooker

2 tablespoons canola oil or bacon grease
2-3 potatoes, chopped
1 large carrot, chopped
1 Bell pepper, chopped
1 stalk celery, chopped
1/2 cup chopped cabbage, broccoli or squash
Enough water to come to top of vegetables
1 cup chopped leftover beef roast, pork roast or chicken
Salt and pepper to taste
1 tablespoon flour or cornstarch
1/2 cup water

Heat oil or bacon grease on medium heat in the deep skillet. Add the potatoes and carrots and other ingredients as you get them ready, adding the meat last. Stir often and add more water as needed. Cook 30 minutes, or until potatoes and carrots are tender. Mix the flour or cornstarch with 1/2 cup water to dissolve and add to the hash, stirring until it begins to thicken. Serve with cornbread.

Tip: Freeze leftover meat in 1 or 2 cup portions in plastic freezer bags. Then it's always ready for a quick week night supper.

"I have never had this dish turn out the same way twice. I clean out the refrigerator and use whatever I have on hand.."

GARDEN MEAT LOAF
Jeanne Mynatt Scholze

1 tablespoon olive oil
1 medium or large onion, finely chopped
1/2 Bell pepper, finely chopped
1 cup grated carrots
1 can (15 oz.) diced tomatoes
1 can (8 oz.) tomato sauce
1/2 cup milk
1 tablespoon Worcestershire sauce
3 eggs
1 1/2 teaspoons salt
1/2 teaspoon pepper
2 slices bread
1/2 cup catsup
2 to 2 1/2 pounds lean ground beef
1/2 pound ground pork
4 slices bacon for garnish
Catsup for garnish.

In skillet, sauté onion, Bell pepper and carrots in olive oil until tender. Add diced tomatoes and tomato sauce and cook over medium-low heat for about 15 minutes. Set aside. In large bowl, beat eggs and add milk, catsup, Worcestershire sauce, salt, and pepper. To this, add the two slices of bread and let soak, then mix well. Into this, mix the ground beef and pork, using hands if necessary. Then thoroughly combine the sautéed onions, pepper, carrots, and tomatoes into the meat mixture. Place in two loaf pans that have been sprayed with cooking spray. Garnish with catsup and bacon slices. Preheat oven to 350° F. Bake for about 1 hour and 15 minutes. Put baking potatoes in at the same time; add a salad and dinner is ready. Serves 8.

Tip: Can be prepared early in the day, or even the night before. Store in the refrigerator in covered glass bowl. Place into cast iron loaf pans when ready to bake.

MUFFIN MEATLOAVES

Youngie Plaster

 2 Lodge
Mini Cake Pan

1 tablespoon cooking oil
1/4 teaspoon minced garlic
1/2 medium onion, chopped
1/2 green pepper, chopped
2 eggs, beaten
1 pound ground beef

1 cup bread crumbs
2 tablespoons A1 sauce
(or favorite meat sauce)
1 teaspoon salt
3/4 cup milk

Preheat oven to 450° F. Place drop biscuit pans that have been generously sprayed with cooking spray in oven to heat. Sauté garlic, onion, and pepper until light brown in skillet with cooking oil. In a mixing bowl, combine all ingredients and mix well. Pack mixture into hot pans, about 3/4 full. Bake for 20 minutes, or until brown. Serve with green beans, whipped potatoes, and cornbread. Children like these small meatloaves.

BEEF AND SAUSAGE CASSEROLE

Alma Fine McCully

 Lodge 5 Qt. Deep
Covered Skillet

2 pounds ground beef
1 pound sausage
1 can (15 oz.) tomatoes, diced
1 teaspoon salt
1 teaspoon oregano
2 small Jalapeno peppers, seeded and finely chopped
8 ounces sour cream
8 ounces cottage cheese
8 green onions with tops, finely chopped
8 ounces small noodles, uncooked
16 ounces Swiss cheese, grated

In deep skillet, brown beef and sausage. Remove from heat and drain. In a bowl or blender, combine tomatoes, salt, oregano, and peppers. Add to the meat mixture in the skillet and simmer 10 minutes. Blend cottage cheese, sour cream, and onion and set aside. Cook noodles, drain and mix the cottage cheese mixture into the noodles. Preheat oven to 325° F. Remove the meat mixture from the skillet. Layer 1/2 noodle mixture into skillet, then 1/2 the meat mixture and repeat layers. Top with grated cheese and bake for 30-35 minutes or until brown on top. Serves 10.

CABBAGE ROLLS
Billie Cline Hill

1 large head cabbage
1 teaspoon salt
1 large onion, chopped
1 tablespoon butter, margarine, or shortening
1 pound ground beef
1/2 pound ground pork or sausage
1 egg, beaten
1 teaspoon paprika
1/2 teaspoon black pepper
1 tablespoon salt
1/2 cup rice, uncooked
2 cans (15 oz.) sauerkraut with liquid
1 can (15 oz.) tomato sauce (or 2 cups homemade)

In Dutch oven, place cored cabbage in enough boiling water (with 1 teaspoon salt) to almost cover cabbage. As leaves wilt, cut them away and remove them from water. Sauté onion in butter and set aside. In large mixing bowl, combine meat, egg, seasonings, onion, and rice and mix well. When all leaves have been removed from the cabbage, pour water from Dutch oven. Put one can of sauerkraut in bottom of Dutch oven and set aside. Remove the thick vein on the back of each cabbage leaf. Place 1 tablespoon of meat mixture into leaf; fold one side of leaf over mixture and roll. Tuck in other end of leaf and secure with toothpick. Place in Dutch oven on top of sauerkraut. Repeat until all leaves are used. Pour the other can of sauerkraut on top of cabbage rolls and top with tomato sauce. Add enough water to cover. Cook two hours on low heat on top of stove.

My husband's aunt, in Newark, Ohio, shared this recipe with me upon our visit just following our marriage in 1951.

CHEESY-BEEFY CORNBREAD

Betty Mayfield Thomas

Lodge
10 1/4 In. Skillet

1 pound ground beef
1 package taco seasoning
1 1/2 cups self-rising cornmeal
1/2 cup self-rising flour
2 eggs
1 can (8 oz.) cream-style corn

1/4 cup canola oil
1 cup milk
1 medium onion chopped
1 cup shredded Cheddar
  cheese
1 Jalapeno pepper, chopped

Lightly grease skillet; place on medium heat and brown ground beef with taco seasoning. Remove from heat; remove meat from skillet and drain. Preheat oven to 325° F. Mix cornmeal, flour, eggs, corn, oil, and milk in a bowl and pour half of mixture into the greased skillet where meat cooked. Top with meat mixture, onions, cheese, and pepper. Pour remaining cornmeal mixture over top. Spread evenly. Bake for 50 minutes. Cool about 15 minutes before cutting and serving. Serves 4.

MEXICAN MEAT WITH CORNBREAD TOPPING

June Chance

Lodge
10 1/4 In. Skillet

1 tablespoon cooking oil
1 pound ground beef
1 teaspoon salt
1/8 teaspoon pepper
1/2 teaspoon chili powder
4 teaspoons grated onion
1 can (15 oz.) stewed tomatoes
2 cups cooked rice

Topping
1 cup cornbread mix
1 egg, beaten
1/2 cup buttermilk

Brown meat in cooking oil in skillet. Add seasonings and tomatoes. Cook and stir until meat and tomatoes are in small pieces. Stir in rice. Cook until thoroughly heated and liquid is absorbed. Preheat oven to 425° F. Add beaten egg to cornbread mix and gradually stir in buttermilk to make thin batter. Top meat mixture with cornbread batter. Bake for 25 minutes. Serves 4.

GARLIC-MINT ROASTED LEG OF LAMB

Jeffrey Logan Cole

3/4 loaf of white bread
1 tablespoon chopped fresh mint
1 pound salted butter, divided
5 pound leg of lamb
15-20 cloves of fresh garlic, peeled and quartered

Horseradish Mint Sauce

1 jar (12 oz.) mint jelly
1 heaping tablespoon Hellmann's mayonnaise
1 teaspoon ground, prepared horseradish

Remove crust from white bread and toast on a cookie sheet until both sides are crisp and brown. Let cool. In a sauce pan, melt butter (1/2 pound to start). Do not allow the butter to separate or clarify. On medium heat, add the melted butter to a skillet along with the mint, and begin crumbling the bread into the melted butter. Add more butter or bread until the mixture maintains a paste-like consistency. Preheat oven to 325° F. Pierce the lamb leg using a small paring knife and insert quarter slices of the garlic cloves into the pierced holes. Evenly distribute the garlic across the entire surface of the lamb leg. Place the leg of lamb in the Dutch oven fat side up. Apply the bread/butter/mint paste liberally to the surface of the lamb, coating all exposed areas with at least 1 inch of the mixture. Cover and place on the middle rack of the preheated oven for approximately 20 minutes per pound or until the internal temperature is 145° F. Cook uncovered for the last 30 minutes. For the horseradish mint sauce, combine mint jelly, mayonnaise, and horseradish in small mixing bowl and whisk until smooth.

BOSTON BUTT PORK ROAST

Lodge 7 Qt.
Dutch Oven

Jeanne Mynatt Scholze

2 tablespoons cooking oil
5 to 7 pound Boston Butt pork roast
2 cups hot water
1 onion, quartered
2 stalks celery, quartered
2 carrots, peeled and quartered
Cavender's Greek seasoning or favorite dry rub

Put oil in Dutch oven and place on top of stove and turn burner to high. Sear each side of roast. When pork roast is browned on all sides, reduce heat to medium-low. Season all sides of roast liberally with Cavender's seasoning. Add 2 cups hot water without pouring over top of roast so not to disturb seasoning. Place onion, celery, and carrots around roast. Cover with lid. (The vegetables are for seasoning and will cook down. If you want to have vegetables to eat, add more about an hour before removing the roast from the oven.) Preheat oven to 325° F. When liquid has reached a simmer, place in oven and bake for 3 to 4 hours. Serves 6-8.

Tip: It works for any other pork or beef pot roast, too. No other cookware does this as well as cast iron.

JOE RAY WILSON'S PORK LOIN

Lodge 5 Qt.
Dutch Oven

Joe Ray Wilson

4 pound lean pork loin
2 tablespoons cooking oil
2 large purple onions, sliced
1 jar mincemeat

Select a nice, lean pork loin and have the butcher saw through the bones at serving size intervals. Put cooking oil in Dutch oven and place on top of stove on medium-high heat. Preheat oven to 350° F. Brown roast on all sides in the Dutch oven. Generously mound roast with sliced onions. Pour a jar of mincemeat over all. Cover and cook in oven 35 minutes per pound (about 2 1/2 hours), until tender. Serves 6-8.

Tip: Allow 1/2 pound for each serving. Mincemeat flavored with rum is best.

FAR EASTERN PORK ROAST

Ed Cobleigh
Paso Robles, California

 Lodge 5 Qt.
Dutch Oven

2 cups chicken stock
1/2 cup dry white wine or cooking sherry
1/2 cup soy sauce
4 tablespoons brown sugar
4 or 5 star anise pods, crushed
4 garlic cloves, minced
1/2 teaspoon Chinese five spice powder
1/4 teaspoon Tabasco sauce
4 pound boneless pork shoulder roast
Salt to taste
Fresh ground pepper to taste
1 tablespoon extra-virgin olive oil
Handful of freshly chopped cilantro
Cooked noodles or rice to serve 6

In a small bowl, mix the chicken stock with the wine, soy sauce, brown sugar, star anise, garlic, five spice powder, and Tabasco. Set aside. Season the pork with salt and pepper. On the stove top, heat the oil in the Dutch oven. Brown the pork on all sides, turning occasionally. Add the sauce mixture and bring to a boil, scraping up any browned bits from the bottom of the pot. Cover and cook in a 350° F oven for 2 to 3 hours, or simmer on the stove top for 2 or 3 hours. Remove the pork, but keep the sauce hot. Discard the strings around the meat. Pull the pork into long strands, then return it to the sauce to reheat. Turn pork and sauce onto a serving dish and garnish with cilantro. Serve over noodles or rice.

"This is a dish that I have served many times in my Lodge Dutch oven. It is pork roast with an oriental flair. I call it Far Eastern (as in the Orient) Pork Roast. The star anise pods and the Chinese five spice powder may be obtained at any oriental market."

SKILLET PORK WITH WILD RICE
Barbara Woodfin

Lodge 3 Qt. Deep
Covered Skillet

1/4 cup chopped green onion
1/4 cup chopped green pepper
2 tablespoons canola oil
1 1/2 cups cooked pork, cut into 3/4 in. cubes
2 cups cooked long grain wild rice
1 jar (2 1/2 oz.) sliced mushrooms, drained
1/2 cup water
2 tablespoons dry white wine
1/2 teaspoon chicken bouillon granules
1/4 teaspoon dried basil
1 tomato, chopped

In skillet, sauté onion and pepper in hot oil over medium heat until tender. Stir in pork, rice, mushrooms, water, wine, bouillon granules, and basil. Bring to a boil and then reduce heat. Cover and cook until most of the liquid is absorbed, about 15 minutes, stirring occasionally. Add tomato and cook over medium heat until thoroughly heated. Serves 4.

Tip: An excellent way to use leftover pork roast.

PAN-FRIED PORK CHOPS
Debbie Clepper Pickens

Lodge
12 In. Skillet

Lodge
12 In. Lid

1/4 cup cooking oil
1 1/2 pounds thin boneless pork chops
1 teaspoon salt, or to taste
1 teaspoon pepper, or to taste
1/2 cup flour

Lay pork chops on wax paper and salt and pepper to taste. Dredge pork chops in the flour. Heat oil in skillet on medium high heat. Fry the pork chops in batches on medium high heat until brown on both sides. Drain on paper towels. Serves 4.

Tip: To fry thicker pork chops, brown the chops, then cover and reduce heat to low for 30 minutes. When chops are tender, remove cover and turn on high to crisp and brown.

SWEET AND SOUR PORK CHOPS
June Chance

 Lodge
12 In. Skillet

6 to 8 thick pork chops
1/4 cup soy sauce
1/4 cup chili sauce
1/4 cup honey

Preheat oven to 350° F. Put pork chops into greased skillet. Mix sauces and honey and pour over pork chops. Bake uncovered for 1 hour. Serves 6.

RED BEANS AND RICE
Billie Cline Hill

 Lodge 7 Qt.
Dutch Oven

2 pounds red beans
1 pound spicy sausage cut into strips
3 medium yellow onions, chopped
6 celery stalks, chopped
4 cloves garlic, minced
1 cup minced parsley
2 tablespoons salt
2 teaspoons cayenne pepper
1 teaspoon black pepper
Cooked rice for 8 servings

Rinse the red beans and soak overnight in a large bowl with water that is several inches above beans. Drain beans, put in Dutch oven and add enough fresh water to cover. Simmer for 1 1/2 hours, checking water level occasionally. In skillet, cook the sausage and add sausage to the beans, leaving drippings in skillet. Sauté onions and garlic in the drippings and add to the red beans. Add celery, parsley, and spices. Simmer for another 1 1/2 hours. To thicken the beans, remove about two cups of beans from the Dutch oven and mash. Return mashed beans to the Dutch oven. Add any additional salt and pepper. Serve over cooked rice with cornbread. Serves 8.

Tip: When making dried beans, don't add salt until beans are tender.

TURKEY AND HAM CASSEROLE

Virginia Loyd

 Lodge 10 1/2 In.
Square Skillets

1/2 cup chopped onion
7 tablespoons flour
7 tablespoons butter, divided
1/2 teaspoon salt
1/4 teaspoon freshly ground black pepper
1 can (4 oz.) sliced mushrooms and liquid
1 cup light cream
4 tablespoons dry sherry
2 cups cubed cooked turkey
1 cup cubed cooked ham
1 can (5 oz.) sliced water chestnuts, drained
1/2 cup coarsely grated Swiss cheese
1 1/2 cups soft bread crumbs

Preheat oven to 400° F. In the skillet, sauté onion in 4 tablespoons butter until tender. Blend in flour, salt, and pepper. Add mushrooms and liquid, light cream, and sherry. Cook and stir until thick. Add turkey, ham, and water chestnuts. Top with cheese. Melt remaining 3 tablespoons of butter and mix with bread crumbs. Sprinkle around edge of casserole. Bake 30 minutes until bubbly hot and light brown. Serves 4.

"This is a delicious dish and a good way to use leftover Thanksgiving turkey and ham."

Soups & Stews

Every Southerner knows that the best cookware comes in one color...black. It is common knowledge that the only kitchen utensil necessary for preparing a great soup or stew is a well-seasoned cast iron pot. It's the black pot that makes the good soup by imparting each successive recipe with the flavors from the memories of meals past. If you are blessed with the cast iron cookware from your mother or your grandmother, then you know that the moment that you begin to heat the pot, you can feel her by your side.

HEARTY LODGE HODGE PODGE

Lodge 5 Qt.
Dutch Oven

Hal Morris
Lookout Mountain, Tennessee

> 2 pounds ground chuck
> 3/4 cup chopped onion
> 1 clove garlic, minced
> 3 cans minestrone soup
> 1 can (31 oz.) pork 'n beans
> 1 cup chopped celery
> 1 tablespoon Worcestershire sauce
> 1/2 teaspoon oregano
> 1 cup water
> 1 cup beef broth
> Salt and pepper to taste

Brown ground beef in Dutch oven, then drain well. Add all other ingredients, stir and heat. Simmer as long as you like, usually about 2 hours.

AFRICAN CHOP

Lodge 7 Qt.
Dutch Oven

Gladys Streeter Wooten

> 2 pounds stew beef, cut into 1 in. cubes
> 3 bouillon cubes
> 2 teaspoons salt
> 1/2 teaspoon crushed red pepper
> 1 teaspoon chili powder
> 2 tablespoons curry powder
> 4 cups water
> 4 slices bacon
> 2 pounds collard greens, washed, drained and thinly sliced
> 1 cup chopped onions
> 1 can (28 oz.) tomato puree

In Dutch oven, place stew beef cubes, bouillon, salt, red pepper, chili powder, curry powder, and water. Stir and bring to rapid boil. Reduce heat and simmer covered for 1 hour. Cut bacon into small pieces and fry in skillet until all fat is rendered. Remove bacon from the skillet and reserve. Sauté greens and onions in fat for 5 minutes, stirring constantly. Add greens, onions, and tomato puree to the stew. Stir and simmer covered for another hour. Garnish with bacon pieces. Serve with rice. Serves 8.

"A traditional New Year's dish served with black-eyed peas."

EASY BEEF STEW

Ann Pickens
Cleveland, Tennessee

Lodge
Combo Cooker

3 tablespoons canola oil
Salt and pepper to taste
1/3 cup flour
1 1/2 pounds beef stew meat
3 cups beef broth, divided
1 large onion, sliced
3 cups sliced carrots
4 medium potatoes, chopped
1/2 cup sliced celery

Put combo cooker on stove top and heat oil on medium. Season meat with salt and pepper, then coat with flour. Put meat in hot oil and brown. Add onions, and 1 1/2 cups of broth. Cover and simmer for 1 1/2 hours or put in oven at 325° F for 1 1/2 hours. Add the remaining broth, carrots, celery, and potatoes and cook 30 minutes, or until tender. Serve with cornbread made in the lid of the combo cooker.

Ann comes from a long line of cast iron cooks. An iron bean pot sits on her stove at all times, and several cast iron skillets adorn the kitchen walls.

GARY'S CABBAGE STEW

Martha Holland

Lodge 5 Qt.
Dutch Oven

1 pound smoked sausage
1 head cabbage, chopped
1 onion, chopped
1 can (28 oz.) diced tomatoes with liquid
1/2 can water
Salt and pepper to taste

Brown sausage in Dutch oven. Add cabbage and onion. Pour tomatoes over all; salt and pepper to taste. Simmer on top of stove or in oven at 350° F for 1 1/2 hours.

Variation: For extra zip, Sara Reed uses 2 cans Rotel tomatoes with green chilies and 3 cups water instead of the diced tomatoes.

OVEN BEEF STEW

Sarah Kirkwood Lodge

 Lodge 5 Qt. Dutch Oven

2 1/2 pounds stew beef
6 carrots, chopped
3 medium onions, quartered
5 medium potatoes, quartered
1 can (28 oz.) whole tomatoes with liquid
1 package (10 oz.) frozen peas
2 bay leaves
2 beef bouillon cubes
Dash of thyme
1 tablespoon salt
1 tablespoon sugar
4 tablespoons cornstarch
Black pepper to taste
1 cup of good red wine or water

Preheat oven to 275° F. Layer beef into Dutch oven. Add vegetables, seasonings, cornstarch, and wine in order listed. Cover with lid and cook for 4 to 5 hours. Stir once or twice.

Tip: Raise the oven temperature to 300° F for slightly shorter cooking time.

CABBAGE BEEF SOUP

Helen Fannelle Clay

 Lodge 7 Qt. Dutch Oven

1 pound ground beef
3/4 cup chopped onion
1/3 cup chopped Bell pepper
3 quarts water
1 can (15 oz.) red kidney beans, rinsed and drained
1 cup beef consume
1 can (6 oz.) tomato paste
3 ounces Worcestershire sauce
1 1/2 pounds chopped or shredded cabbage

In skillet, cook ground beef and drain. Put into Dutch oven with remaining ingredients. Cook on medium heat until done. Season with salt and pepper to taste.

JESSE'S CAMP STEW SOUP

Lodge 9 Qt.
Dutch Oven

Jesse Reed
Former maintenance supervisor at Lodge

1/4 cup corn oil
2 or 3 pounds chuck roast, cut in cubes
4 large potatoes, quartered
2 large onions, sliced
1 whole garlic bulb, peeled and sliced
2 or 3 Jalapeno peppers, chopped
2 small cans sliced mushrooms
1 can (10 oz.) Rotel tomatoes and green chilies
1 can (28 oz.) tomatoes with liquid
1 can (15 oz.) whole kernel corn
1 can (15 oz.) green peas
2 cans Veg-All
2 1/2 quarts water
1 teaspoon salt
1/2 teaspoon black pepper

Heat oil until hot in a very large pot. Add beef and stir-fry about 5 minutes. Add remaining ingredients and bring to full boil. Reduce heat and slow boil for 3 or 4 hours. Keep watch to be sure it doesn't stick or boil over. Serves a big bunch of hungry hunters.

TACO SOUP
Mary Jo Teeters Walker

2 pounds lean ground beef
2 large onions, chopped
2 cans (15 oz.) Mexican-style chili beans with liquid
1 can (15 oz.) black beans with liquid
1 can (15 oz.) white whole kernel corn with liquid
1 can (11 oz.) Mexican-style corn with liquid
2 cans (14 oz.) chicken broth
1 can (15 oz.) tomato sauce
1 can (28 oz.) diced tomatoes with liquid
2 cans (10 oz.) Rotel tomatoes with green chilies
1 package taco seasoning
1 package Ranch dressing mix
Shredded Cheddar cheese for garnish
Tortilla chips for garnish

In Dutch oven, brown ground beef. Drain well. Add onions and cook until tender. Add other ingredients and cook (uncovered) for about 45 minutes. Ladle into serving bowls and top with cheese and tortilla chips. Easy dish for a large group.

Tip: If too thick, add 2 more cans chicken broth.

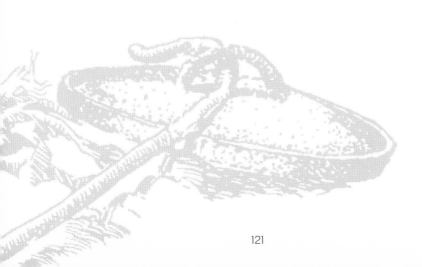

BRUNSWICK STEW
Barbara Gonce Clepper

2 pounds cooked chicken
2 1/2 pounds cooked pork
2 cans (15 oz.) whole kernel yellow corn
2 cans (15 oz.) butter beans
3 cans (15 oz.) diced tomatoes
2 large onions, chopped
32 ounces chicken broth
1 bottle (24 oz.) of ketchup
1/2 cup vinegar
1/2 cup Worcestershire sauce
1/4 cup brown sugar, firmly packed
1 tablespoon salt
1 tablespoon pepper
2 tablespoons hot sauce

Chop chicken and pork into bite-size pieces and put in Dutch oven. Add all remaining ingredients. Cover and simmer, stirring occasionally, for 3 hours. Makes about 25 cups. Serves 12.

TENNESSEE WHITE CHILI

Lodge 5 Qt.
Dutch Oven

Mike Gonce

1 1/2 pounds cooked chicken breasts
1 tablespoon canola oil
1 teaspoon minced garlic
1 cup chopped onion
3 cans (15 oz.) great northern beans, drained
2 teaspoons cilantro or 2 tablespoons chopped fresh cilantro
2 teaspoons cumin
1/4 teaspoon salt
1/4 teaspoon cayenne pepper
Shredded Monterey Jack cheese for garnish
Tortilla chips, crushed, for garnish

Chop chicken into small cubes. Heat oil in Dutch oven. Cook onion and garlic over medium heat until tender. Stir in remaining ingredients, except cheese and chips. Heat 30 minutes. Serve sprinkled with cheese and crushed tortilla chips. Serves 6.

Tip: Recipe can easily be doubled to serve a crowd. Use 7 Quart Dutch Oven.

SOUTHERN GREENS SOUP

Lodge 7 Qt.
Dutch Oven

Louise S. "Lou" Fuller, wife of Ed Fuller
First President of the National Cornbread Festival

1 medium onion, chopped
2 tablespoons cooking oil
4 cups water
1 package Knorr's dry vegetable soup mix
2 pounds fresh turnip greens, washed, drained, and chopped
1 can (20 oz.) white beans, drained
1 package Polish sausage, sliced

Sauté onion in oil in Dutch oven. Add water and vegetable soup mix. Bring to a boil and simmer for 5 minutes. Add turnip greens and simmer uncovered for 10 minutes. Add white beans and sausage. Simmer, uncovered, for about 15 minutes until greens are tender. Add more hot water if you want it more "soupy". Serve with hot cornbread. Serves 4.

TEXAS-STYLE CHILI

Mary Jo Teeters Walker

 Lodge 5 Qt.
Dutch Oven

3 pounds boneless stew beef, cut into 1/2 in. cubes
(or substitute 3 pounds lean ground beef)
1 1/2 cups chopped onion
1 cup chopped Bell pepper
3 cloves garlic, minced
2 cans (28 oz.) diced tomatoes
2 cups water
1 can (6 oz.) tomato paste
8 beef bouillon cubes
2 tablespoons chili powder
1 tablespoon ground cumin
2 teaspoons crushed oregano leaves
2 teaspoons sugar

In Dutch oven, brown beef. If using ground beef pour off fat. Add onion, Bell pepper, and garlic. Cook and stir until tender. Add remaining ingredients. Cover and bring to boil. Reduce heat and simmer 1 1/2 hours (1 hour for ground beef) or until beef is tender. Serve with corn chips and shredded cheese, if desired. Makes about 4 quarts.

Tip: For chili with beans, add 1 can red kidney beans (not drained) just before serving, but then it isn't Texas chili.

CORN CHOWDER
Coughlin Haverty Cooper

 Lodge 3 Qt. Deep
Covered Skillet

5 bacon slices
1 red Bell pepper, chopped
1 medium yellow onion, chopped
1 large russet potato, diced
2 packages (10 oz.) frozen
   shoepeg corn, thawed

1 can (15 oz.) chicken broth
1/2 teaspoon kosher salt
1/2 teaspoon white pepper
1 cup half and half cream

Cook bacon in deep skillet on medium heat until crisp. Remove
bacon, reserving drippings in pan. Drain bacon on paper towels,
crumble, and set aside. Sauté red Bell pepper, onion, potato,
and 1 package of corn in reserved bacon drippings until tender
(approximately 10-12 minutes). Stir in chicken broth, salt, and
pepper. Bring to a boil. Reduce heat and simmer, covered, for 20
minutes. Puree the other package of corn with the half and half
in a blender until smooth. Pour into vegetable mixture. Add bacon
pieces and cook over low heat until thoroughly heated, stirring
constantly. Yields 2 quarts.

MCNEW'S OKRA STEW
Alex at Walden Farm

 Lodge 3 Qt. Deep
Covered Skillet

1 package (10 oz.) frozen baby lima beans, cooked
3 tablespoons canola oil
1 pound okra, ends removed and sliced
1/2 pound smoked sausage, sliced
1 cup chopped onion
1/2 cup chopped Bell pepper
1/2 cup chopped green onions
2 cloves garlic, minced
1/4 teaspoon salt
1/2 teaspoon pepper
1/2 pound shrimp, peeled and deveined
1 can (15 oz.) tomatoes, chopped
Cooked rice for 4

In deep skillet, sauté okra, sausage, onion, Bell pepper, garlic, salt,
and pepper in oil. Cook on medium heat until okra is crisp-tender.
Add shrimp and cook on low heat until shrimp are done, about 5
minutes. Add tomatoes and cook 10 minutes. Add lima beans and
simmer another 15 minutes. Serve over hot rice. Serves 4.

SHRIMP JAMBALAYA

Mary Miles Cameron Grider

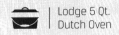

Lodge 5 Qt.
Dutch Oven

1 1/2 pounds medium shrimp, peeled and deveined
2 tablespoons olive oil
1 onion, chopped
1/2 cup chopped Bell pepper
1 carrot cut into thin strips
1/2 cup chopped celery
3 cloves garlic, minced
1 can (8 oz.) tomato sauce
1 can (10 oz.) diced tomatoes and green chilies with liquid
1 can (15 oz.) chicken broth
1 1/4 cups water
1 cup long grain rice, uncooked
1 teaspoon salt
1/2 teaspoon dried thyme
1/2 teaspoon ground red pepper
1/4 teaspoon chili powder
1/4 teaspoon sugar
1/2 cup chopped fresh parsley
Hot sauce for garnish

Cook shrimp in olive oil in Dutch oven over medium heat, stirring constantly about 5 minutes or until shrimp turn pink. Remove shrimp and refrigerate. Add onion, Bell pepper, carrot, celery, and garlic and cook over medium heat for 3 minutes. Stir in tomato sauce and remaining ingredients, except for parsley and shrimp. Bring to a boil, cover and reduce heat. Simmer, stirring frequently, for 45 minutes or until rice is tender and most of liquid is absorbed. Stir in parsley and shrimp. Cook about 10 minutes until thoroughly heated. Serve with bottled hot sauce.

TENNESSEE VALLEY JAMBALAYA

John Richard "Dick" Lodge, Jr

1 small whole chicken
8 links of sweet or hot Italian sausage
3 tablespoons olive oil
1 cup chopped onion
1 cup chopped Bell pepper
2-4 cloves garlic, minced
1 cup country ham cut into bite-size pieces
1 can (15 oz.) whole tomatoes with liquid
1 cup long grain rice, uncooked
1 1/2 cups chicken broth, reserved
1/2 teaspoon thyme
1/2 to 1 teaspoon chili powder
1 1/2 teaspoons salt
1/2 teaspoon freshly ground black pepper
1 1/2 tablespoons chopped fresh parsley

Cook chicken until tender in enough water to cover (about 30 to 40 minutes). Cool chicken and reserve chicken broth. Tear or cut chicken into bite-size pieces. Preheat oven to 350° F. Cook Italian sausage in oven until brown and cooked through (about 30 minutes). Cool until able to handle and cut sausage into 1/8 inch slices. In Dutch oven sauté onion, Bell pepper, and garlic in olive oil until just tender. Add chicken, sausage, and ham. Add tomatoes, rice, chicken broth, thyme, chili powder, salt, and pepper. Bring to a boil, stirring once or twice. Cover tightly and bake in oven for about 1 hour. If rice is still slightly crunchy, stir and bake 10 to 15 minutes longer. Stir in chopped parsley. Serves 6.

Serve with hot sauce, country-style bread and green salad.

Vegetables

In a time when real estate was more abundant, grocery stores were fewer, and people lived off the land, no homestead was without a vegetable garden. Certainly, no Southern home could survive the winter months without an abundant supply of vegetables in their root cellar and canned in their pantry. The abundance of vegetables led to an abundance of ways to prepare them so that we didn't notice when there was no meat on the table because "pickins were slim". Even today, there is not a Southerner alive who doesn't cherish a meal of fried green tomatoes, fried okra, pinto beans, summer squash, parsley potatoes, green beans, fresh picked corn on the cob, turnip greens, coleslaw, and sliced Vidalia onions. Add a skillet full of hot cornbread, and we are in heaven!

JIMMIE'S RED HOT APPLES

Jimmie Russell

Lodge
8 In. Skillet

1/2 stick margarine
1 cup brown sugar
1/4 cup white sugar
1 tablespoon Cinnamon Red Hots
Enough apples to fill 8 in. skillet

Melt margarine in the skillet. Wash and slice the apples into the skillet. Cover with sugar and start cooking on low heat, stirring often. Cook slowly as mixture makes its own juice. Cook until tender. Stir in Red Hots to add color and flavor. Serve hot or cold.

"I'm lucky to have my own apple orchard on South Pittsburg Mountain. The Winesap or Rome Beauty apple is the best. At eighty two years old, I still pick my own apples (with some help) to make this dish for church and family gatherings." - 2003

OACIE'S BAKED BEANS

Oacie Lee Hart Haney
Hixson, Tennessee

Lodge 5 Qt.
Dutch Oven

1 pound great northern beans
1 medium onion, chopped
1 1/2 teaspoons dry mustard
1 1/2 teaspoons salt, or to taste
3 slices bacon cut into 1 in. pieces

In large bowl, soak beans overnight or at least 6 hours in twice as much water as beans. Drain and rinse until clean. Place in Dutch oven and cover with water to 1 inch above beans. Add all other ingredients and stir well. Cover and bake in 350° F oven for 3 hours. Reduce heat to 200° F and bake 3 more hours, or until done. If more water is needed during baking, add boiling water.

Over 76 years ago, Oacie was given an iron Dutch oven as a wedding present by one of her brothers. At age 89, she was still using the same Dutch oven. Since it had been quite a while since she had used this recipe, she cooked a pot to be sure she still remembered the ingredients. The recipe takes a long time, but is worth the effort. - 2003

COON CREEK BEANS
Pat Frame

Lodge 5 Qt.
Dutch Oven

1 pound great northern beans
1 large onion, chopped
1 large clove garlic, minced
1 tablespoon sugar
1 ham bone
1 cup chopped ham
1 Polish sausage cut in small chunks
1 teaspoon parsley flakes
Salt and pepper to taste

In large bowl, soak beans overnight in at least twice as much water as beans. Drain and rinse beans. Cook beans with ham bone, onion, and garlic in only as much water as needed to barely cover beans. It takes about 1 1/2 hours for beans to become tender. When done, add sugar, parsley, salt, pepper, ham, and Polish sausage. Let simmer a few minutes to heat through.

Tip: Serve with Green Tomato Relish, Mexican cornbread, and salad.

FRIED GREEN BEANS
Frances Porter

Lodge
9 In. Skillet

1 can (14.5 oz.) Allen's green beans
2 strips bacon

Drain beans. Fry bacon in skillet until crisp. Crumble bacon and return to skillet. Add beans to skillet and brown. Serve with cornbread and sliced tomatoes.

"Several families from Tuscumbia, Alabama always enjoy stopping in South Pittsburg to shop at Lodge's Factory Store on their way to the Great Smoky Mountain National Park. They always talk about the quaint, old buildings of South Pittsburg."

HERBED GREEN BEANS
Mary Jo Teeters Walker

 Lodge
12 In. Skillet

6 slices bacon
1 cup sliced mushrooms
1 cup chopped onions
1 clove garlic, minced
2 tablespoons chopped fresh parsley
 or 1 tablespoon dried parsley
2 tablespoons bacon drippings
2 cans (16 oz.) Blue Lake green beans, drained
1/2 teaspoon salt
1/4 teaspoon rosemary
1/4 teaspoon marjoram
1/2 teaspoon black pepper

In skillet, fry bacon. Crumble and set aside. Remove all but
2 tablespoons bacon drippings from skillet. Sauté mushrooms,
onions, garlic, and parsley in bacon drippings. Stir drained beans
into sautéed mixture with remaining seasonings and simmer
20 minutes. Top with crumbled bacon before serving.

SOUTHERN STYLE STRING BEANS
Jeanne Mynatt Scholze

 Lodge 5 Qt.
Dutch Oven

About 2 pounds green beans
About 1/2 pound October beans, shelled
1/2 pound salt pork
Salt to taste

Wash green beans, remove strings and break into small pieces.
Rinse the shelled October beans. Put pork into Dutch oven, which
is about 1/2 full of water. Bring to a boil. Add the green beans
and October beans. Cover and cook slowly until the water has
all boiled away and the beans are tender, about 3 hours. Salt to
taste and serve with hot cornbread.

STELLA'S GREEN BEANS

Stella Harris

 Lodge 7 Qt.
Dutch Oven

Enough green beans to fill Dutch oven
Chunk of salt pork or ham
Large onion, chopped
Salt to taste
Fresh vegetables
  (a few okra pods, some squash, a few potatoes,
  or whatever is on hand)

Wash green beans, remove strings and break into small pieces. Add prepared green beans, onion, and salt pork to Dutch oven. Put in enough water to come near the top of beans. Cover and cook slowly until the water has cooked down some. Now, lay any fresh vegetables you wish on top of beans. Continue cooking until the vegetables are done and water is almost gone. Total cooking time is about 2-3 hours.

Tip: Serve with tomatoes, onions, and cucumbers from the garden with hot cornbread muffins.

CABBAGE CASSEROLE

Louis Fuqua

 Lodge 3 Qt. Deep
Covered Skillet

2 medium onions, chopped
1 small Bell pepper, chopped
1 clove garlic, minced
1/4 cup unsalted butter
2 1/2 cups Cheddar cheese, shredded and divided
1 large cabbage, chopped, cooked, and drained
1 cup bread crumbs
Salt and pepper to taste
1 cup half and half cream

Preheat oven to 350° F. Sauté onion, Bell pepper, and garlic in butter in deep skillet. Add cabbage, 2 cups cheese, bread crumbs, salt, and pepper. Mix well. Top with 1/2 cup cheese and pour half and half over the top. Bake for 30-40 minutes.

CORN PUDDING
Virginia Loyd

Lodge 10 1/2 In.
Square Skillets

1/4 cup butter
1/4 cup flour
2 teaspoons salt
1 1/2 tablespoons sugar
1 3/4 cups milk
3 cups fresh or frozen corn
3 eggs, beaten until frothy

Preheat oven to 350° F. Melt butter in skillet. Stir in flour, salt, and sugar. Cook until bubbly. Add milk and cook until thick. Stir in the corn, either chopped or whole kernels, but chopped makes a smoother pudding. Stir in the eggs that have been beaten until frothy. Pour into greased skillet and bake for about 45 minutes.

Tip: If not baking in cast iron, bake in a hot water bath.

FRIED CORN
Gladys Streeter Wooten

Lodge
10 1/4 In. Skillet

6 large ears fresh corn (yellow or white)
3 tablespoons bacon grease
1 tablespoon flour
1 tablespoon sugar
1/2 cup milk
1 cup water
3 tablespoons butter
Salt and pepper to taste

Remove kernels from corn with a sharp knife. Put bacon grease in skillet and heat. Combine corn, flour, sugar, milk, and water. Add corn mixture to hot bacon grease. When mixture is hot, add butter, salt, and pepper. Stir and cook until corn is tender. Serve 4.

BILLIE'S FRIED EGGPLANT
Billie Cline Hill

Lodge
12 In. Skillet

1 large eggplant
2 tablespoons flour
1/2 teaspoon baking powder
1 egg, beaten
1/2 cup milk
Cornmeal for dredging
Enough cooking oil to fill skillet 1/4 in. deep

Peel eggplant and slice into rounds about 1/2 inch thick. Put in bowl filled with cold, salted water and soak about an hour. Rinse and drain for about 30 minutes. In another bowl, combine flour, baking powder, egg, and milk. Put cornmeal on plate or wax paper. Add cooking oil to skillet and heat on medium until hot. Dip eggplant slices in the egg batter, and then dredge in cornmeal. Place eggplant slices in hot oil and fry until golden brown. Drain on paper towels. Serves 3-4.

Tip: Also a wonderful batter for fried green tomatoes.

"This batter recipe is from my Aunt Grace and is the best one I've found. She only cooked in cast iron until the day she died at 102 years old."

EGGPLANT AU GRATIN
Virginia Loyd

Lodge 10 1/2 In.
Square Skillets

4 small or 2 large eggplants, peeled and chopped
2 large onions, chopped
1 stick butter, divided
2 eggs, beaten
3 cups grated Cheddar cheese
Salt and pepper to taste
1/2 cup cracker crumbs

In saucepan, boil eggplant in salted water until tender. Drain, mash, and drain again, if necessary. Use the skillet to sauté the onions in half of the butter. Preheat oven to 350° F. Combine eggplant, onions, eggs, cheese, salt, and pepper. Place in greased skillet. Top with cracker crumbs and dot with remaining butter. Bake for 45 minutes. Serves 8 to 10. For a smaller family, halve the recipe and cook in 6 inch skillet.

ITALIAN EGGPLANT PARMESAN

Major Jayne Clepper Halvorson, Retired

2 medium eggplants
1 cup milk
1 1/2 cups Italian seasoned bread crumbs
1/2 cup olive oil
2 cans (10 oz.) Rotel Italian diced tomatoes
2 cans (10 oz.) Rotel diced tomatoes and green chilies
2 tablespoons chopped fresh basil, divided
3/4 cups grated fresh Parmesan cheese
2 cups grated Mozzarella cheese, divided

Peel and slice eggplants. Dip slices into milk, and dredge in bread crumbs. In batches, fry eggplant in hot olive oil in skillet over medium heat for 2-3 minutes on each side. Remove from skillet and cool on a wire rack. Preheat oven to 400° F. Process Italian diced tomatoes in blender until smooth. Stir in drained diced tomatoes and green chilies and 1 tablespoon chopped basil. Pour half of tomato sauce into greased skillet. Top with half of the eggplant slices. Sprinkle with half of the Parmesan and half of the Mozzarella cheeses. Repeat sauce, then eggplant. Bake for 15 minutes. Top with remaining cheeses and bake 5 more minutes. Sprinkle with remaining basil before serving. Serves 6-8.

"The U.S. Army spent a fortune moving my vast collection of Lodge cast iron all over the country and to Germany 3 times. I couldn't cook without it."

SOUTH COAST HOMINY
Carolyn Gonce LeRoy

Lodge
10 1/4 In. Skillet

3 tablespoons butter
1 small onion, minced
1/2 cup chopped Bell pepper
3 tablespoons flour
1 teaspoon salt
1/2 teaspoon dry mustard
Dash cayenne pepper
1 1/2 cups milk
1 cup grated Cheddar cheese
1/2 cup chopped pitted ripe olives
1 can (28 oz.) yellow hominy, drained
1/2 cup buttered bread crumbs

Preheat oven to 375° F. Melt butter in skillet. Add onion and green pepper and sauté for 5 minutes. Blend in flour and seasonings. Add milk and cook, stirring constantly until mixture thickens and comes to a boil. Add grated cheese and stir until melted. Remove from heat and add olives and hominy. Sprinkle with buttered bread crumbs. Bake 30 minutes or until brown.

"Every fall in the late 1930s, Edith Lodge Kellermann would send her son Leslie, down to the Joseph Lodge farm, where I was born, to get corn for making their hominy. Leslie later became president of Lodge."

SOUTHERN FRIED OKRA

Beth Duggar
President of the National Cornbread Festival

Lodge
12 In. Skillet

2 quarts okra
1 to 2 eggs, beaten
1 cup cornmeal (approximately)
1 teaspoon salt, or to taste
1/4 teaspoon pepper, or to taste
1/2 - 3/4 cup bacon drippings, enough to fill skillet 1/4 in. deep

Wash okra in sink with lots of water. Let okra dry. Remove ends and slice into 1/4 to 1/2 inch segments into a bowl. If okra is tough, throw it out. Pour the egg(s) over the okra and mix it up so the okra is coated with the egg. Mix the cornmeal into the okra. Salt and pepper to taste. Put the bacon drippings into skillet and heat on medium-high heat until hot. To test, place one slice of okra in skillet to see if it really sizzles. Pour the breaded okra into skillet and cook until golden brown, turning with a spatula. Some people like it almost burned. (More bacon grease may be needed.) Serves 4-6 people that love okra.

Variation: Add 1/2 teaspoon onion powder or garlic powder when seasoning.

Tip: Cooking oil may be substituted for bacon grease. It's just not as good!

Freezing Tip: Take okra straight from the garden and put it directly into freezer bags. When ready to use, thaw and wash. This way the okra holds its "slime" which is what makes it great!

FRIED OKRA FINGERS
Mildred Walker Clepper

Lodge 3 Qt.
Deep Skillet

Lodge
Fry Basket

20 very small okra pods
1 cup buttermilk
3/4 cup all purpose flour
1/4 cup cornmeal
1 teaspoon baking powder
1/2 teaspoon salt
Dash of pepper
Cooking oil for filling deep fryer

Wash okra and remove stems/caps. Drain well and place in a shallow container with the buttermilk. Set aside. Combine flour, cornmeal, baking powder, salt, and pepper. Mix well. Remove okra pods from buttermilk and roll in cornmeal mixture. Drop into deep hot oil and fry 3-5 minutes, turning once. Drain on paper towels.

VIRGINIA'S STIR-FRIED OKRA
Virginia Loyd

Lodge
12 In. Skillet

1/4 cup vegetable oil
1 pound fresh okra, ends removed and sliced
1 large onion, finely chopped
1 large Bell pepper, seeded and finely chopped
1 cup chopped celery
1/4 teaspoon salt
1/4 teaspoon pepper
1/2 teaspoon thyme
3 tablespoons soy sauce

Heat oil in skillet on medium-high until hot. Combine okra with onion, Bell pepper, celery, salt, pepper, and thyme. Add okra mixture to skillet and stir fry about 8-10 minutes, or until okra is crisp tender. Add soy sauce to vegetable mixture and cook stirring constantly until okra is tender.

GOURMET ONIONS

Judy Atnip Clepper

Lodge
10 1/4 In. Skillet

> *5 medium Vidalia onions, sliced*
> *1/2 teaspoon sugar*
> *1/2 teaspoon salt*
> *1/2 teaspoon pepper*
> *1/3 cup butter*
> *1/2 cup dry sherry*
> *1/4 cup grated Parmesan cheese*

Combine onions, sugar, salt, and pepper. Melt butter in skillet and add onion mixture. Cook for 8 minutes, stirring frequently. Stir in sherry and cook for 3-4 more minutes. Sprinkle with cheese and serve. Serves 6.

POKE SALAT

Louis Fuqua

Lodge
12 In. Skillet

> *2 gallons fresh picked young poke*
> *4 cups water*
> *1/2 cup chopped green onions*
> *3 tablespoons bacon grease*
> *Salt to taste*
> *1 egg, beaten*

Wash poke greens and put in pot with water. Bring to a boil, stir down and boil 5 minutes. Drain and rinse greens. Return to pot; add onions and 1 cup water. Boil for 20 minutes, covered. Drain again. Melt grease in skillet on medium heat; add poke greens and salt. Stir fry 5 minutes. Add beaten egg and cook until egg is done. Serve with cornsticks.

Tip: Pick poke in April. It grows wild near the edges of fields, along fence lines and roadways.

COUNTRY-FRIED POTATOES

Frances Porter

Lodge
12 In. Skillet

Lodge
12 In. Lid

> *2 tablespoons canola oil or bacon drippings*
> *4 medium potatoes, peeled and sliced*
> *1 medium onion, sliced*
> *Salt and pepper to taste*

Put oil in large skillet. When oil is hot, add the potatoes, onions, and seasonings. Cook with lid on until tender. Remove lid and brown on both sides. Serve hot.

DUTCH OVEN POTATOES
Jimmie Henson

 Lodge 7 Qt.
Dutch Oven

5 pounds potatoes, cut into wedges
2 sticks butter or margarine
3 medium onions, cut into wedges
Dash garlic salt
2 bay leaves
Celery salt to taste
Salt and pepper to taste
Basil to taste (and any other seasoning that you like)

Preheat oven to 250° F. Place onions, butter, potatoes, and seasonings in Dutch oven. Cover and bake in oven about 3 hours, or until tender. Serves 12.

Tip: One third of recipe fits into 2 Quart Serving Pot and serves 3-4.

POTATO PANCAKES
June Beene Chance

 Lodge
12 In. Skillet

Enough cooking oil to fill skillet about 1/4 in. deep
4 potatoes, peeled, grated, and drained
1 onion, grated
1 teaspoon salt
1/4 teaspoon pepper
1 egg, beaten
5 tablespoons self-rising flour

Heat oil in skillet until hot. Mix all ingredients in a bowl. Drop by heaping tablespoonful into hot skillet. Fry until golden brown, turning with spatula.

Variation: Use 1 1/2 cups leftover mashed potatoes instead of grated potatoes.

"A simple recipe that is best in a cast iron skillet."

CASSEROLE RICE
Carolyn Kellermann Millhiser

> 1/4 cup butter or margarine
> 1/4 cup chopped onions
> 2 cups raw rice
> 3 cups water
> 2 sprigs parsley, minced
> 1 bay leaf
> 1/4 teaspoon dried thyme leaves
> Salt to taste

Preheat oven to 400° F. Melt butter in Dutch oven on top of stove. Add onion and cook until wilted. Stir in rice, water, herbs, and salt. Bring to a boil. Cover and place in the oven. Bake 25 to 30 minutes until rice has absorbed the liquid. Remove bay leaf before serving.

Variation from Shirley B. DeWitt: Use beef consomme instead of water and add 1 can mushrooms. She has named it Holly's Rice because it is one of her daughter's favorite recipes.

FRIED RICE
Mary Jo Teeters Walker

> 1 cup chopped onion
> 3 tablespoons vegetable oil or sesame oil
> 2-3 cups cooked diced pork, ham, chicken, or turkey
> 4-6 cups day-old steamed rice
> 2-4 tablespoons soy sauce
> 2 eggs, slightly beaten
> 1/2 cup grated carrots
> 1-2 cups English peas, cooked and drained

Brown onion in deep skillet. Add meat and carrots and heat thoroughly. Add rice and toss until heated throughout. Sprinkle with soy sauce. Pour eggs over mixture. When eggs begin to coagulate, toss until well mixed. Flatten the top of the mixture. Place peas on top of the rice mixture. Cover and simmer a few minutes on low heat. Serves 4 to 8.

MARY JANE'S BLACK SKILLET RICE AND ALMONDS

Mary Jane Joyner Brown
Former Co-Chairman of the South Pittsburg
Historic Preservation Society

Lodge 3 Qt. Deep
Covered Skillet

> 1 1/2 cups uncooked rice
> 2 cans beef consomme
> 2 cans water
> 3/4 stick butter
> 1 small package blanched slivered almonds
> Salt and pepper to taste

Preheat oven to 350° F. Melt butter in deep skillet. Add rice and brown very slowly, stirring constantly. When rice is browned, add almonds, salt, and pepper. Pour in liquids. Cover with lid of deep skillet and bake for 1 hour. Stir and bake uncovered for 30 minutes. Serves 8 to 10. Good with Barbecue chicken.

SKILLET SQUASH

Jeanne Mynatt Scholze

Lodge
12 In. Skillet

Lodge
12 In. Lid

> 3 pounds yellow summer squash and zucchini,
>   sliced into 1/2 in. slices
> 1 medium onion, chopped
> 3 tablespoons butter
> 1 tablespoon sugar
> 1 teaspoon sage
> 2 eggs, slightly beaten
> 1 cup cheese, cubed (Velveeta melts best)
> Crushed crackers or dressing mix for topping

Preheat oven to 350° F. In skillet, melt butter and sauté onion until tender. Add squashes, sugar, and sage. Cover, but check and stir frequently until squash is almost tender. Remove from heat. Add cheese and stir. Add eggs and stir. The mixture should be cool enough so eggs do not begin to cook when added. Add topping and place in oven and bake for about 25 minutes until set. Serves 8.

STIR-FRIED RICE
Dr. James Blackman Havron

2 cups uncooked rice
3 cups water
3 strips bacon cut into pieces
Bacon drippings reserved from cooking bacon
6-8 shrimp cut into bite-sized pieces
2 eggs, slightly beaten
Pinch of salt
1 tablespoon oil
1 cup frozen green peas, thawed and drained
3-4 green onions, chopped
3 tablespoons catsup

Prepare the rice by washing 5 times; then drain. In a sauce pan, add water to the rice and bring to a boil until it bubbles. Cover the rice and remove the pot from heat briefly while turning the heat down low. Return to heat and cook for 20 minutes. Take off the heat and lightly fluff with a fork. Fry the pieces of bacon in wok until crispy. Remove to paper towel. Remove the drippings and reserve for later use. Fry the shrimp pieces in the hot wok until pink. Remove cooked shrimp to a paper towel.

To the wok add a pinch of salt, then softly scramble the eggs. Remove eggs and set aside. Place bacon drippings plus oil in the hot wok and add 3 to 4 cups of the cooked rice and stir-fry for 3-4 minutes. Add the peas and cook 1 minute. Turn off heat. Add all remaining prepared ingredients, then fold the green onions and catsup into the mixture. Can be used as a main course or served with other foods.

SQUASH CASSEROLE

Charlotte and Dallas Durham

2 pounds yellow crookneck squash, diced (8 medium)
1 large onion, chopped
1 Bell pepper, chopped
4 eggs, beaten
1/2 pint whipping cream
1/2 pound Cheddar cheese, grated
24 Ritz crackers
1 teaspoon sugar
1/2 teaspoon seasoned salt
1 teaspoon salt
1/2 pound butter, divided
4 slices bread for topping

Cook squash, drain well and mash. Sauté onion and pepper in
1/4 pound butter. Remove from heat. Preheat oven to 350° F.
Roll crackers into crumbs and add to squash. Mix in onion, Bell
pepper, grated cheese, seasoned salt, sugar, salt, and cream.
Add eggs and mix well. Put squash mixture in skillet. Toast bread
and roll to make crumbs. Melt butter in melting pot and add to
bread crumbs. Spread topping on squash mixture. Bake for 35-45
minutes. Serves 8.

SQUASH CHESTNUT CASSEROLE
Mildred Walker Clepper

3 pounds yellow summer squash
Salt and pepper to taste
3 eggs, beaten
2 tablespoons sugar
2 tablespoons butter
1/2 cup evaporated milk
1 cup chopped onions
1 can (8 oz.) water chestnuts, drained and chopped
3/4 cup crumbled soda crackers
1 1/2 cups grated Cheddar cheese

Topping
3/4 cup crushed soda crackers
1/2 cup butter, melted

Cook squash in boiling water until tender. Drain. Preheat skillet in
375° F oven. Beat eggs and mix with the other ingredients. Mix
egg mixture into squash. Pour into hot, greased skillet. Top with
remaining cracker crumbs and melted butter. Bake for 30 minutes
until lightly brown. Serves 8.

*"Squash is best just picked from the garden next door. Even
at 84, I have not gotten too old to pick vegetables and try out
new recipes." -2003*

SUMMER SQUASH CASSEROLE

Lynda King Kellermann

 Lodge 2 Qt.
Serving Pot

2 pounds yellow squash, sliced
1 small onion, finely chopped
4 tablespoons butter
Salt and pepper to taste
1/3 cup sugar
2/3 cup cream
1 egg, beaten
4 soda crackers

Boil squash and onion in small amount of water until tender, about 7 minutes. Preheat oven to 350° F. Drain squash and onion well. Mash with potato masher. Add butter, seasoning to taste, sugar, milk, and egg. Pour into greased serving pot. Crumble cracker crumbs on top. Bake 30-40 minutes until firm. Serves 6.

CANDIED SWEET POTATOES

Faye Marsh

 Lodge
10 1/4 In. Skillet

2 large sweet potatoes
1/2 stick margarine
1 cup sugar
1/2 cup cream

Peel sweet potatoes and slice fairly thin. Melt margarine in skillet. Place potatoes in margarine. Add sugar and small amount of water. Cook on low heat until tender, about 30 minutes. Syrup should thicken and potatoes should be tender when tested with a fork. Remove slices with spatula and place on platter. Add cream to syrup in skillet and let it cook until it thickens. Pour over potatoes.

"I grew up on a farm in Roane County, Tennessee where we grew our own sweet potatoes. This remains one of my favorite recipes." - 2003

ESTELLE'S FRIED SWEET POTATOES

Estelle Peoples

Lodge
10 1/4 In. Skillet

Lodge
10 1/4 In. Lid

2 or 3 sweet potatoes
2 tablespoons oil
1 or 2 tablespoons water, more if needed
1/2 teaspoon salt
2 cups sugar
4 tablespoons butter or margarine

Peel and slice sweet potatoes long-wise. Place oil in skillet on medium heat. When oil is hot, add potatoes, water, salt, and sugar. Cover and cook until tender. Watch to be sure they don't burn. Turn very carefully when needed, but do not stir, as this causes them to be mushy. Add butter and let it melt and blend with sugar mixture. Serve hot.

Estelle, now in her 90s, didn't measure when she cooked. She made a special effort to cook this recipe and measure as she went so she could contribute. - 2003

HOLIDAY SWEET POTATOES

Patsy Ambrester Sherrill

Lodge 10 1/2 In.
Square Skillets

3 cups cooked and mashed sweet potatoes
1 cup sugar
2 eggs, beaten
1/4 cup milk
1 can (3.5 oz.) coconut
1 teaspoon salt
1 teaspoon vanilla
1/2 cup margarine, melted

Topping
1 cup brown sugar
1/4 cup margarine, melted
1 cup chopped pecans

Preheat oven to 350° F. Mix sweet potatoes, sugar, eggs, milk, coconut, salt, vanilla, and margarine. Pour into greased skillet. Bake for 20 minutes. Combine brown sugar, pecans, and margarine to make topping. Sprinkle on sweet potato dish. Bake an additional 20 minutes until brown. Serves 8.

ISABELLE'S SWEET POTATO CASSEROLE

Georgia Isabelle Millard Bishop

3 cups cooked and mashed sweet potatoes
1 cup sugar
2 eggs, beaten
1/2 cup milk
1/2 teaspoon salt
1 teaspoon vanilla

Topping

1 cup brown sugar   *1 cup chopped pecans*
1/2 cup flour   *1/2 stick butter, melted*

Preheat oven to 400° F. Mix sweet potatoes, sugar, eggs, milk, salt, and vanilla. Pour into greased skillet. Combine brown sugar, flour, pecans, and butter to make topping. Sprinkle on casserole. Bake 30-40 minutes until brown. Serves 6-8.

Tip: Dish may be cooked in a pastry shell and served as dessert.

FRIED GREEN TOMATOES

Ann and Wayne Gray

4 large green tomatoes   *1/2 cup bread crumbs*
2 eggs   *2 teaspoons coarse kosher salt*
1/2 cup milk   *1/4 teaspoon ground pepper*
1 cup flour   *Vegetable oil (to fill skillet*
1/2 cup cornmeal   *1/2 In. deep)*

Slice tomatoes 1/2 inch thick. Whisk eggs and milk together in a medium bowl. Scoop flour onto a plate. Mix cornmeal, bread crumbs, salt, and pepper on another plate. Put oil in skillet and heat on medium heat until hot. Dip tomatoes into flour to coat, then into the milk and egg mixture. Dredge in bread crumbs to completely coat. Then place tomatoes into the skillet in batches of 4 or 5. Do not crowd the tomatoes. They should not touch each other. When the tomatoes are brown, turn and fry on the other side. Drain on paper towels.

Variation: Use 1 1/2 cups flour instead of cornmeal and bread crumbs. Follow steps above except after battering the tomatoes, refrigerate them on a covered plate for 30 minutes before frying. This holds the batter on the tomatoes.

GREEN TOMATO BAKE
Louis Fuqua

8 medium green tomatoes,
 (peeled and cut into 3/4 in. slices)
1/2 cup grated Parmesan cheese
1 1/2 cups fine bread crumbs
1 teaspoon salt
1/4 teaspoon pepper
4 tablespoons butter

Preheat oven to 350° F. Put half of the tomato slices into the skillet. Mix cheese, bread crumbs, salt, and pepper. Sprinkle half of the mixture over the tomatoes in the skillet. Dot with butter and top with remaining tomato slices and the rest of the crumb mixture. Bake for about 50 minutes.

MUDDIE'S GREEN TOMATO RELISH
Cheryl LeRoche Kellermann
wife of Bob Kellermann, CEO of Lodge

2 quarts chopped green tomatoes (about 6-8)
3 green Bell peppers, chopped
3 red Bell peppers, chopped
5 large onions, chopped
3 tablespoons salt
3 cups cider vinegar
2 1/2 cups sugar
2 tablespoons celery seed
1 tablespoon whole allspice
1 tablespoon tumeric

Combine tomatoes, peppers, and onions. Sprinkle with salt and let sit for 30 minutes. *Drain well*. Place all other ingredients plus vegetables in large pot and bring to a boil. Stir down and boil for a second time. Ladle into hot mason jars and seal. Makes approximately 6 pints.

"This recipe was passed down from my grandmother to my mother to me."

ZUCCHINI CHEESY FRITTERS

Emily LeRoy

Lodge 3 Qt.
Deep Skillet

Lodge
Fry Basket

1 1/2 cups flour
1 cup chopped zucchini
1/2 cup shredded Cheddar cheese
1/4 cup finely chopped onion
1 egg, beaten
1 cup milk
Canola oil to fill deep fryer about 1/2 full

Mix ingredients together just enough to moisten well. Heat oil
in deep fryer until bubbling hot. Drop by rounded tablespoon
into hot oil. Cook only a few at a time, turning once, until lightly
browned and cooked through. Drain on paper towels. Serve hot.
Serves 4.

ZUCCHINI PIE

Carolyn Kellermann Millhiser
daughter of Charles Richard "Dick" Kellermann
third president of Lodge from 1949-1974

Lodge 10 1/2 In.
Square Skillets

3 cups unpeeled diced zucchini
1 large onion, chopped
1/2 cup grated Parmesan cheese
1/2 cup grated Cheddar cheese
1/2 cup salad oil
1 cup Bisquick baking mix
4 eggs, beaten
3-4 tablespoons minced parsley
1 teaspoon salt
1/2 teaspoon pepper

Preheat oven to 350° F. Combine all ingredients, mixing until
zucchini is coated with batter. Pour into greased skillet. Bake 35-
40 minutes until light brown. Serves 12. Freezes well.

Variation: A small can of sliced, drained mushrooms may be
added for variety.

Desserts

Southerners certainly own no patent on having a sweet tooth. Perhaps, we are not the only group still having old-fashioned covered dish suppers. This is a treat that should be enjoyed by one and all. Where else can one sample an array of luscious homemade cakes, pies, cookies, fudge, pralines, and custards – each lovingly offered as the signature dish of it's respective contributor.

JULIA CLINE'S JAM CAKE

Billie Cline Hill

3 Lodge
10 1/4 In. Skillets

2 cups sugar
1/2 cup butter
3 cups flour
6 egg yolks
2 cups buttermilk
2 teaspoons baking soda
2 teaspoons cinnamon
2 teaspoons cloves
2 teaspoons nutmeg
2 teaspoons allspice
3 tablespoons cocoa
2 cups jam, usually blackberry
1 cup raisins

Preheat oven to 325° F. Line skillets with wax paper because the cake has a tendency to stick because of the jam. Cream butter and sugar, then add egg yolks one at a time. Set aside. In another bowl, mix buttermilk and baking soda for 3 minutes. Add flour and buttermilk alternately, then add other ingredients. Pour into 3 skillets and bake for 30 minutes.

Filling
1 cup milk
2 cups sugar
1/2 cup butter
Pinch of baking soda

Combine milk, sugar, butter, and soda in deep skillet (must be cast iron or it won't turn out). Cook about 20 minutes until mixture forms a ball in cold water or reaches the hard ball stage on a candy thermometer. Place filling between layers of cake.

"This recipe was handed from my great grandmother to my grandmother to my mother to me. Jam cake was usually a winter cake, made when there was little fresh fruit available. I still have the original paper written in my great grandmother's hand on January 1, 1900. My grandmother made notes in the margin about only using cast iron for the icing and doubling the icing recipe."

AMARETTO PECAN CAKE

Carolyn Gonce LeRoy

1/2 cup chopped pecans
1 box yellow cake mix
1 package (3.5 oz.) vanilla pudding and pie mix
4 eggs
1 stick butter, melted
1/2 cup oil
1/2 cup water
1/2 cup amaretto

Sauce

1 stick butter
1 cup sugar
1/4 cup amaretto

Preheat oven to 325° F. Grease and flour fluted cake pan. Crumble pecans into bottom of pan. Place cake mix and pudding mix in bowl. Add eggs, butter, oil, water, and amaretto. Mix 2 minutes. Pour batter into pan, only filling about 2/3 full. Bake for 50 minutes or until done. Make sauce just before the cake is done.

To make sauce, slowly heat butter and sugar in small saucepan until sugar is dissolved. Remove from heat and add amaretto. Stir to mix well. While cake is still in pan and piping hot, punch lots of tiny holes all over cake and pour half of sauce over cake. Let cool and invert onto plate and pour the remaining sauce over the top of the cake. Freezes well.

Variation: You may use rum or wine instead of amaretto.

JO BAILEY CAKE
Coughlin Haverty Cooper

1 cup unsalted butter
2 cups sugar
3 eggs
2 1/2 cups cake flour

3/4 cup cocoa
1/2 cup cold, strong coffee
1/2 cup buttermilk
1 teaspoon baking soda

Preheat oven to 350° F. Grease and flour 2 skillets and set aside. Cream butter and sugar in mixing bowl. Add eggs one at a time, beating well after each addition. Sift cake flour, cocoa, and baking soda several times into a separate bowl. Then slowly mix flour mixture into batter. Add remaining ingredients, mixing well. Divide batter equally between skillets and bake for 30 minutes.

Fudge Icing

2 cups sugar
1/2 cup unsalted butter
2 squares unsweet chocolate

1/2 cup milk
1 teaspoon vanilla

For the icing combine ingredients **except** vanilla in a cast iron skillet. Bring to a boil, stirring constantly. Cook for one additional minute. Remove from heat and add vanilla. Beat until thickened. (Icing should be used immediately – it hardens quickly!)

"When the Tennessee Valley Authority brought power to the Sequatchie Valley, local homemakers gained the ability to cook with electricity. Electric ovens became all the rage, and the Electric Power Board provided an instructor to teach the ladies how to operate their new stoves. A class was held at Rogers Furniture Store and Miss Jo Bailey taught the baking of this cake in an electric oven. Louise Rogers attended the seminar and she passed the recipe to her friend Isabelle Bishop who, in turn, shared it with her neighbor across the alley, Agnes Gentry (my grandmother). Agnes baked the cake for many years, then my mother continued the tradition. The Jo Bailey Cake is more than a list of ingredients to my sister, Holland and me; it is a special part of our heritage. We loved to share this "slice of home" and its story with our dorm-mates in college. It is in keeping with the southern tradition of passing recipes from generation to generation, from Tennessee to Mississippi, from backyard to backyard across the fence."

AUNT CRICKET'S SOUR CREAM CAKE

Billie Cline Hill

Fluted
Cake Pan

1 stick margarine
1 stick butter (be sure to use one of each)
3 cups sugar
6 large eggs
2 tablespoons vanilla
3 cups flour, sifted
1/4 teaspoon baking soda
1/4 teaspoon baking powder
1/4 teaspoon salt
1 cup sour cream

Preheat oven to 325° F. Cream butter, margarine, and sugar together. Add one egg at a time (turn bowl to side and beat each egg well making sure white is well beaten), then fold into batter. Repeat for each egg. Add vanilla. Sift flour, salt, baking soda, and baking powder together. Add flour mixture and sour cream alternately until all is beaten in. Beat vigorously until smooth. Pour into a well-greased and floured fluted cake pan or tube pan and bake for one hour. Test with broom straw or toothpick for doneness. Remove from pan after cake has cooled for 15 minutes.

CHARLOTTE'S FRUIT CAKE
Charlotte Durham

Fluted
Cake Pan

1 pound candied cherries, chopped
1 pound candied pineapple, chopped
4 cups chopped pecans
2 cups self-rising flour
1/2 pound butter
1 cup sugar
5 eggs, lightly beaten
1 tablespoon vanilla
1 tablespoon lemon juice

Grease and flour cake pan. Mix fruit and nuts together and coat with flour. Set aside. In mixing bowl, cream butter and sugar together. Then add beaten eggs, vanilla, and lemon juice. Pour into fruit and nut mixture and mix well. **Put in cold oven** and bake for 2 1/2 hours at 300° F.

HERSHEY CAKE
Debbie Pickens

Fluted
Cake Pan

8 regular Hershey candy bars
8 ounces Hershey chocolate syrup
2 cups sugar
1 cup buttermilk
1/2 teaspoon baking soda
2 teaspoons vanilla
4 eggs
2 1/2 cups plain flour, sifted
2 sticks butter, softened

Preheat oven to 325° F. Melt candy bars and syrup, being careful not to scorch. Add vanilla to mixture and set aside. In another bowl, cream butter and sugar. Add eggs one at a time, beating well after each. Add cooled chocolate to butter mixture. Combine baking soda and flour. Alternately add flour mixture and buttermilk into chocolate mixture. Mix well. Pour into greased and floured pan. Only fill pan 2/3 full. Pour any leftover batter into small loaf pan. Bake 1 1/4 hours. (The small loaf pan will only take an hour.) Cool 15 minutes before removing from pan. Very moist and delicious!

Tip: If you have enough batter to bake additional small loaf pan, freeze. Makes excellent hostess gift.

BANANA FRUIT CAKE

Gaynelle Reed

Fluted
Cake Pan

1/4 pound butter (no substitutes)
1/2 cup Wesson oil
2 cups sugar
4 eggs, well beaten
6 ripe bananas, mashed
1/2 cup raisins
2 cups chopped pecans
1/2 pound candied cherries (optional)
3 cups flour, divided
2 teaspoons baking soda
1 1/2 teaspoons ground cloves
1/2 teaspoon salt
2 1/2 teaspoons cinnamon

Preheat oven to 350° F. Spray cake pan with Baker's Joy. Cream butter, oil, and sugar. Add beaten eggs and mashed bananas. In another bowl, coat raisins, pecans, and cherries in 1/2 cup flour. Sift together the remaining flour, baking soda, spices, and salt. Add slowly to the banana mixture. Blend well. Fold in the fruit and nuts. Pour batter into the pan, only filling it about 3/4 full. Bake for about an hour. Let cool about 15 minutes before removing from pan. It is very important to wait 3 days or longer before cutting this cake. Keep it covered and store in the refrigerator.

MOMMA CLINE'S FRESH APPLE CAKE

Billie Cline Hill

Fluted
Cake Pan

Lodge
9 In. Skillet

2 cups sugar
1 1/2 cups cooking oil
2 teaspoons vanilla
3 eggs, well beaten
Juice of 1/2 lemon (about 1 1/2 tablespoons)
1 teaspoon salt
1 1/4 teaspoons baking soda
2 teaspoons baking powder
1 teaspoon ground allspice
1 teaspoon ground cinnamon
3 cups flour
3 cups peeled and chopped apples
1 cup chopped pecans

Preheat oven to 325° F. Grease and flour pan. Peel and chop apples. As you peel, drop apples into cool, salted water to keep them from turning brown. (Drain well when ready to use.) Combine sugar, oil, vanilla, eggs, lemon juice, and salt in large bowl. Beat well. Mix baking soda, baking powder, spices, and flour. Add flour mixture to first mixture and beat well. Add apples and pecans. Pour into pan, filling only 2/3 full. Bake for 1 1/2 hours. Leave in the pan and glaze with the following.

Glaze

1 cup brown sugar, packed
1 stick margarine
1/4 cup milk
1 teaspoon vanilla

Mix and cook in skillet for 2 1/2 minutes. Pour over cake while hot. Let cake cool in pan.

Tips: If you have too much batter for cake pan, use a small loaf pan for the leftover batter, cooking for 1 hour until done. May need to cover with foil last 30 minutes to keep from getting too brown. (Good even without glaze.)

MARY SUE'S POUND CAKE

Doris Marsh Durham

2 or 3 Lodge
Loaf Pans

1 cup butter
3 cups sugar
5 eggs
3 cups flour (sifted 3 times before measuring)
1 teaspoon salt
1 teaspoon baking powder
2 teaspoons vanilla
1 cup whipping cream

Grease and flour loaf pans. Cream butter and sugar together. Add eggs one at a time, beating after each addition. Add flour slowly, mixing well. Add salt, baking powder, vanilla, and whipping cream. Pour into loaf pans, filling only 2/3 full. *Start in cold oven,* then bake at 325° For 1 hour and 20 minutes or until it tests done.

Variation: Libby Austin uses 7 eggs and says it was Elvis Presley's favorite cake.

"On Saturday afternoons we baked cookies, cakes, and made candy. Mary Sue Gentry and I would put a cake in the oven at my house and then go to Mary Sue's and bake one there. Then we would go back to my house and make icing for both cakes. After we were grown, Mary Sue always blamed me because she couldn't make icing, since I had always made it for both of us."

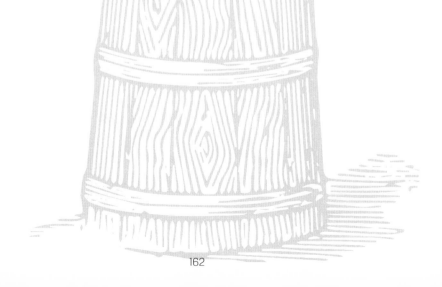

COCONUT POUND CAKE

Jeanne Mynatt Scholze

Fluted
Cake Pan

2 sticks butter
1/2 cup Crisco shortening
3 cups sugar
6 eggs
3 cups flour
1 cup milk
Dash salt
1/2 teaspoon almond flavoring
1/2 teaspoon coconut flavoring
1 bag (7 oz.) flaked coconut, divided

Cream butter with Crisco and sugar. Add eggs, one at a time, beating after each egg. Alternately add flour and milk. Beat in salt and flavorings. Fold in about 4 or 5 ounces of the coconut. Pour into well-greased and floured pan. **Start in cold oven,** then bake at 350° F for 1 hour and 10 minutes. Let cake cool about 15 minutes before removing from pan. While cake is cooling in the pan, make sauce.

Sauce

1/2 cup water
1 cup sugar
1 teaspoon coconut flavoring

Put all ingredients into a saucepan and boil and stir 1 minute. When cake has been removed from the pan, but is still hot, poke holes in the top and spoon the hot sauce over the cake. It should absorb into the cake. When about half of the hot liquid is left, garnish the top of the cake with the remaining coconut, then continue spooning liquid over it. Do not cut until the next day.

PINEAPPLE UPSIDE DOWN CAKE
Faye Marsh

Lodge
10 1/4 In. Skillet

Topping
1 can (20 oz.) crushed pineapple
2 cups brown sugar, firmly packed
1/4 cup butter
1/2 teaspoon salt

Cake
1 cup sugar
1/2 cup margarine
2 eggs
1 3/4 cups flour, sifted 3 times
3 teaspoons baking powder
1/4 teaspoon salt
1/2 cup milk
1 teaspoon vanilla

Preheat oven to 325° F. In the skillet, cook the pineapple, brown sugar, butter, and salt until the topping thickens slightly. Set aside. In a mixing bowl, cream sugar and margarine. Add eggs one at a time, beating well after each. Combine dry ingredients in another bowl. Gradually add dry ingredients and milk to the mixture, alternately. Add the vanilla. Mix well. Pour batter by spoonfuls over the pineapple mixture in the skillet. Bake for about an hour or until the cake tests done. Turn out onto large plate and cut into wedges. Serves 8 to 10.

Variation: You can use sliced pineapple "for looks", but Faye notes that the crushed pineapple is better.

"I make this cake in an iron skillet purchased from Lodge in 1932, the year that Ed Marsh and I moved to South Pittsburg. It was a "second" and has no numbers on it, but it is probably a number 8. Ed paid 38 cents for it. That black iron skillet has never rusted and remains slick as a ribbon. I would love to see everything that I have cooked in it for the last 70 years. That is a lot of Good Eating!" - 2003

PINEAPPLE UPSIDE DOWN CAKE

Lodge
12 In. Skillet

Elizabeth Rogers Kelly
Elizabeth Adams
Lynda King Kellermann

Topping

1 cup brown sugar
3 tablespoons butter or margarine
7 slices pineapple rings (canned)
Maraschino cherries

Cake

3 eggs
1 1/2 cups sugar
1 teaspoon vanilla
1/2 cup pineapple juice (from pineapple rings)
1 1/2 cups flour
1 1/2 teaspoons baking powder
1/4 teaspoon salt

Preheat oven to 350° F. In the skillet, melt butter over low heat. Sprinkle the brown sugar over the butter. Remove from heat. Arrange pineapple rings in the skillet. Place a cherry in the center of each ring. Mix eggs and sugar in a mixing bowl. Add vanilla and pineapple juice. Combine flour, baking powder, and salt. Add to the batter. Pour batter over pineapple rings in the skillet. Bake 45 minutes until nicely brown. Turn out on platter while warm. Serves 8 to 10.

Variation: Pecans or walnuts and/or raisins added to the topping make cake "prettier and tastier".

ORANGE CAKE

Donna Cook Lodge
wife of Henry Ware Lodge, President of Lodge

Fluted
Cake Pan

Lodge
9 In. Skillet

1 package lemon Jell-O pudding mix
3/4 cup Wesson oil
1 package DuncanHines Orange Supreme cake mix
3/4 cup water
4 eggs
1 teaspoon vanilla extract
1 teaspoon almond extract

Preheat oven to 325° F. Grease and flour cake pan. Combine lemon Jell-O pudding mix and Wesson oil. Mix in cake mix and water. Add eggs and extracts. Blend well. Pour into cake pan and bake for about 1 hour or until it tests done.

Sauce

2 cups powdered sugar
1 cup orange juice
2 tablespoons butter
2 tablespoons Grand Marnier

Melt butter on low heat in skillet. Add remaining ingredients and heat gently. While still warm, dribble over the top of warm cake.

"When I was a student at the University of the South, I met Henry Lodge, already an alumnus. One of his favorite teachers was his former psychology professor, Charles Peyser, who invited students to his home and often served this orange cake (Henry's favorite). When Henry and I married, Professor Peyser included the recipe in his wedding gift. Just this year (2002), our daughter Masey attended Professor Peyser's psychology class at the University of the South. Both he and his cake are still favorites at our house."

SOUR CREAM COFFEE CAKE

Lynda King Kellermann

Fluted
Cake Pan

1 cup butter	2 cups flour
2 cups plus 4 teaspoons sugar	1 teaspoon baking powder
2 eggs	1/2 teaspoon salt
1 cup sour cream	1 cup chopped pecans
1/2 teaspoon vanilla	1 teaspoon cinnamon

Preheat oven to 350° F. Grease and flour pan. Cream butter and add 2 cups of the sugar gradually, beating until light and fluffy. Beat in the eggs one at a time very well. Fold in cream and vanilla. Sift flour, salt, and baking powder together in separate bowl. Fold flour mixture into batter. Combine 4 teaspoons sugar with cinnamon and nuts. Place about 1/3 of the batter into pan. Sprinkle with 3/4 of the pecan mixture. Spoon in the remaining batter and sprinkle with remaining pecan mixture.
Bake about 60 minutes or until done. Cool on a rack.

Before baking, cut across batter with a knife to remove air pockets.

MATHEW'S CUPCAKES

Jayne Clepper Halvorson

4 Lodge
Muffin Pans

1 cup shortening
2 cups sugar
4 eggs
3 cups cake flour
2 1/2 teaspoons baking powder
1/2 teaspoon salt
1 cup milk
2 teaspoons pure vanilla

Preheat oven to 375° F. Grease muffin pans. Beat shortening at medium speed with electric mixer until fluffy. Gradually add sugar, beating well. Add eggs, one at a time, beating well after each. In another bowl, combine flour, baking powder, and salt. Add flour mixture to shortening mixture alternately with milk. Beat at low speed after each addition. Stir in vanilla. Spoon batter into muffin pans, filling them only 1/2 full. Bake for 20 minutes. Remove and cool on wire racks. Spread with caramel frosting. Makes 48 cupcakes.

CARAMEL FROSTING

Jayne Clepper Halvorson

Lodge 3 Qt. Deep
Covered Skillet

1/2 cup butter
1 cup brown sugar, packed
1/4 cup dark corn syrup
2 teaspoons cream of tartar
3 cups powdered sugar, sifted
3 tablespoons whipping cream
2 teaspoons pure vanilla

Melt butter in deep skillet over medium-high heat. Stir in brown sugar, corn syrup, and cream of tartar. Bring to a boil and boil for 5 minutes without stirring. Remove from heat and stir in powdered sugar, whipping cream, and vanilla. Beat at medium speed with electric mixer for 2 minutes. Spread on cupcakes immediately.

"This makes a nice hard frosting that children won't get all over themselves and everything else."

CARAMEL ICING

Wilma Houston Kirkpatrick
known affectionately as "Miss Pinkie"

Lodge 3 Qt. Deep
Covered Skillet

3 cups sugar, divided
1 stick margarine
1 cup milk
1 teaspoon vanilla
Pinch of baking soda (maybe 1/8 teaspoon)

In saucepan, put 2 1/2 cups sugar, milk, soda, and margarine. Bring to a boil. Meanwhile, brown 1/2 cup sugar in iron skillet. Slowly pour the contents of saucepan into skillet of browned sugar, stirring constantly. Boil 7 minutes. Take off heat and let cool. Add vanilla and beat until thick enough to spread on cake.

Tip: Cooked icing is difficult to make on humid and rainy days.

FLAKY PIE PASTRY

Lynda King Kellermann

3 cups flour
1 teaspoon salt
1 teaspoon sugar
1 cup shortening (Crisco)
1 egg
Milk

Sift dry ingredients together into large mixing bowl. Add shortening and combine with a pastry cutter (or two table knives). Cut shortening into dry ingredients until the pieces are about the size of a pea. Place egg in a cup, add enough milk to make 1/2 cup and beat slightly to mix. Slowly add milk and egg mixture. Roll the mixture into two balls for two 9 inch pie crusts or three balls for three small crusts. Chill 30 minutes before rolling.

Tip: This pie crust, wrapped in wax paper and then in aluminum foil, will keep for 4 days in the refrigerator or for up to 3 weeks in the freezer.

Tip about pastry: Too much flour makes pie crust tough. Too much shortening makes pastry dry and crumbly. Too much liquid makes pastry heavy and soggy.

BAKED MERINGUE

Stella Harris

3 egg whites
1/4 teaspoon cream of tartar
1/4 teaspoon vanilla extract
1/4 teaspoon almond extract
1/8 teaspoon salt
1/2 cup sugar

Preheat oven to 350° F. Have egg whites at room temperature. Beat egg whites until foamy in a large glass or metal bowl at high speed with an electric mixer. Sprinkle cream of tartar, flavorings, and salt over egg whites. Continue beating until soft peaks form. Gradually add sugar, 1 tablespoon at a time, beating until stiff peaks form. Pipe or spread meringue into desired shapes on the pie filling. Bake until the meringue peaks are slightly brown.

APPLE PIE
Lynda King Kellermann

Lodge
10 1/4 In. Skillet

2 pastry crusts
5-6 cups pared, finely chopped apples
1 cup sugar
1/2 teaspoon cinnamon
1/2 stick butter or margarine, melted in Melting Pot

Preheat oven to 350° F. Line skillet with a pastry. Stir cinnamon into sugar. Alternate layer of apples with layer of sugar mixture. Add melted butter last. Add top sheet of pastry crust. Cut slits or other decoration in top crust to allow steam to escape. Bake on middle rack of oven with foil on the bottom rack to catch spills that happen when pie is baking. (It's very messy!) When pie has cooked for about 20-30 minutes, cover the edges with aluminum foil to keep them from becoming too brown. Total baking time 45-60 minutes, or until brown.

Tip: Tart apples are best for pies, like Granny Smith apples.

Tip: To keep apples from discoloring while you peel, put a little salt in water and drop apples into it after peeling.

Tip: Should any juice spill over into the oven, sprinkle spill with salt to prevent smoke and smell.

"During World War II, Dick and Lynda turned their backyard and the Kellermann family tennis court into a Victory Garden. After the war, they planted apple trees and a pear tree so that the pies and preserves were not only homemade but also homegrown. Lynda always said that Dick could eat a whole pie in two days."

BUTTERSCOTCH PIE
Stella Harris

Lodge 3 Qt. Deep Covered Skillet

1 pie pastry (9 in. or 10 in.), baked
2 1/2 cups sugar, divided
5 egg yolks, beaten
2 tablespoons butter
4 heaping tablespoons flour
4 cups milk
1 teaspoon vanilla

Preheat oven to 350° F. On stove top, brown 1 cup sugar in small iron skillet. Don't let it get too brown or it will be bitter. Melt butter and warm milk in deep skillet. Add 1 1/2 cups sugar, egg yolks, and flour. Cook and stir on medium heat until it begins to get thick. Add caramelized sugar slowly to milk mixture. Stir until sugar dissolves and mixture is very thick. Pour into baked pie shell. Top with meringue (see Baked Meringue recipe) and bake until the meringue peaks are lightly brown.

PECAN PIE
Sarah Kirkwood Lodge

Lodge
Chef Skillet

1 pie pastry (9 in.), unbaked
3 eggs
1 cup white corn syrup
1/2 cup brown sugar
1/4 cup melted butter or margarine
1/8 teaspoon salt
1 teaspoon vanilla
1 cup chopped pecans

Preheat oven to 350° F. Melt butter in Melting Pot and set aside to cool. Prepare pie shell and place in skillet. Combine ingredients in mixing bowl and pour into unbaked pie shell. Bake for about 40 minutes.

Tip: Top should feel soft to touch and middle should shimmy. Filling firms as it cools.

CHOCOLATE CREAM PIE
Deborah Roberts Bonner

 Lodge 3 Qt. Deep
Covered Skillet

1 pie shell (9 in.), baked
2 cups milk
2 squares (1 oz.) unsweetened chocolate
1/3 cup flour or 1/4 cup cornstarch, sifted
1 cup granulated sugar
1/4 teaspoon salt
3 egg yolks, slightly beaten
2 tablespoons margarine
1/2 teaspoon vanilla

Meringue
3 egg whites
1/4 cup sugar
Pinch salt

Heat milk and chocolate together over low heat. Stir frequently. Remove from heat when chocolate is melted. Combine flour, sugar, and salt in a deep skillet. Add chocolate milk mixture gradually. Cook and stir over low heat until mixture boils. Cook two minutes. Remove from heat and stir a little hot mixture into egg yolks. Add yolks to the other hot mixture and stir over low heat until very thick. Remove from heat and stir in butter and vanilla. Cool. Spoon into baked pie shell. Preheat oven to 350° F. Beat egg whites. Add salt and sugar slowly to make meringue. Spoon onto pie. Bake until meringue is lightly brown.

"This recipe was handed down to me by my grandmother, Polly Seward, over 40 years ago."

CHOCOLATE SKILLET PIE
Pauline Clepper

Lodge 3 Qt.
Deep Skillet

1 deep (8 in.) pie shell, baked
1 cup sugar
1 rounded tablespoon flour
3 tablespoons cocoa
3 egg yolks
1 cup milk
1 heaping tablespoon butter
1 tablespoon vanilla

Meringue
3 egg whites
6 tablespoons sugar

Mix together sugar, flour, and cocoa. Set aside. Slightly beat egg yolks in another mixing bowl and add milk. Melt butter in the deep skillet, then stir in the sugar, flour, cocoa mixture. Remove from heat and stir in the liquids. Return skillet to heat and cook on medium heat until very thick. This will take about 15 to 20 minutes. Add vanilla. Pour into baked pie crust. Preheat oven to 325° F. To make meringue, beat egg whites until stiff in a glass or metal mixing bowl. Beat in sugar, one tablespoon at a time. Spread over pie. Bake until meringue is lightly brown.

"This is an often requested favorite at family gatherings."

APPLE DESSERT
Sarah Kirkwood Lodge

1 1/2 cups sugar
1/2 cup butter or margarine
2 eggs
Pinch of salt
1 1/2 cups flour
1 teaspoon cinnamon
1 teaspoon nutmeg
Dash of ground cloves
1 teaspoon baking soda
3 cups sliced and peeled apples

Topping
2 tablespoons butter, melted
3 tablespoons milk
1 1/2 cups brown sugar

Preheat oven to 350° F. Cream sugar and butter. Add the next 7 ingredients and mix well. Add the apples last. Put in skillet. Bake for 25 minutes. Remove from oven and cover with the topping (do not cool beforehand). Return to oven and bake for an additional 25 minutes. Serve warm or cold with whipped cream.

"My husband's service as an Episcopal priest has taken us many wonderful places. One of my favorite times was our stay in Alaska. This recipe is from an Alaskan friend."

DELIGHTFUL APPLE CRISP

Barbara Gonce Clepper

4 cups sliced apples
1/4 cup bought apple juice
3/4 cup flour
1/2 cup sugar
1/2 cup brown sugar
1 teaspoon cinnamon
1/2 teaspoon salt
1/3 cup butter
1/2 cup oatmeal, uncooked

Preheat oven to 350° F. Place apples and apple juice in a greased skillet. Sift flour, white sugar, cinnamon, and salt into a mixing bowl. Cut in butter until mixed well. Add brown sugar and oatmeal to the flour mixture. Sprinkle mixture over the apples. Bake 40 minutes or until apples are tender. This can be served for breakfast or with ice cream as a dessert.

"Being born on the Joseph Lodge farm, I developed a passion for cooking in cast iron and collecting both recipes and cast iron early in life."

BLACKBERRY COBBLER

Bertha Russell Gonce

1 1/4 cups flour, divided
1 1/2 teaspoons baking powder
1/4 teaspoon salt
1/2 cup butter, plus 3 tablespoons
1 cup sugar, divided
1 egg
1 cup milk
1 teaspoon vanilla
3 cups fresh, unsweetened blackberries
1/2 teaspoon cinnamon

Preheat oven to 375° F. Combine 1 cup of flour, baking powder, and salt. Set aside. In a mixing bowl, beat together 1/2 cup butter and 1/2 cup sugar until fluffy. Add the egg and beat. Combine milk and vanilla and add with dry ingredients to the butter mixture. Pour into a greased 10 1/4 inch skillet. Spoon the berries over the batter. Combine the remaining 1/2 cup sugar, 1/4 cup flour, cinnamon, and 3 tablespoons butter. Mix until crumbly. Sprinkle over the berries. Bake for 35 minutes. Good topped with ice cream or whipped cream.

"We have blackberries growing beside the fence in front of our house. We pick them in July, but we have to watch out for ticks, chiggers and snakes." For over 75 years Bertha cooked a big dinner every day at 11:30. Now at 100 years young, she has reluctantly passed the mixing spoon to the next generation. This cobbler is a favorite dessert at Bertha's table."

TENNESSEE BREAD PUDDING

Jeanne Mynatt Scholze

 Lodge
13 1/4 In. Skillet

1 stick butter
1 long loaf French bread, preferably stale
4 cups milk
4 eggs, beaten
2 cups sugar
1 cup raisins
2 tablespoons vanilla

Sauce

1 stick butter
3/4 cup sugar
1 egg, beaten
1/4 cup Jack Daniels, or to taste (rum flavoring can be substituted)

Preheat oven to 350° F. Melt butter in 13 1/4 inch skillet in oven. Tear French bread into pieces. Combine remaining ingredients in large mixing bowl. Add crumbled bread and mix together, mashing with hands if necessary. Pour mixture into bubbling butter in skillet. Bake for 40 minutes, or until center starts getting firm. Near the end of the baking time, prepare the sauce. Melt butter in 10 inch skillet over low heat. In small mixing bowl, combine egg, sugar, and bourbon. Pour into melted butter. Stir and cook until well blended. Pour onto hot pudding.

SKILLET DATE BALLS

Mary Jo Teeters Walker

 Lodge 3 Qt. Deep
Covered Skillet

1/2 cup butter or margarine
1 cup sugar
1/2 pound dates, chopped
2 egg yolks, beaten
1 teaspoon vanilla
2 cups crisp rice cereal
Flaked coconut

Mix butter, sugar, dates, and egg yolks in a skillet. Cook over medium-high heat until mixture begins to boil. Then cook for an additional 10 minutes over medium heat, stirring constantly. Remove from heat and add the vanilla and rice cereal. Shape mixture into small balls and roll each ball in the coconut.

STRAWBERRY PIZZA
Betty Thomas

 Lodge 14 In.
Baking Pan

First Layer
2 cups flour
2 sticks melted butter
1 cup chopped pecans

Second Layer
1 package (8 oz.) cream cheese
1 carton (8 oz.) Cool Whip
1 1/2 cups powdered sugar

Third Layer
3 cups fresh strawberries
1 carton or package strawberry glaze

Preheat oven to 350° F. Mix flour, butter, and pecans together and make crust. Spread on baking pan and bake 15 minutes or until golden brown. Let cool. Mix cream cheese, Cool Whip, and powdered sugar together. Spread over crust. Slice strawberries and add glaze. Spread this over second layer.

MRS. TURNEY'S FUDGE
Billie Cline Hill

 Lodge 3 Qt. Deep
Covered Skillet

3 cups sugar
1 cup evaporated milk
1 stick butter, no substitute
Scant 1/2 cup semi-sweet chocolate morsels
Dash of salt
2-3 tablespoons white Karo syrup
2 teaspoons vanilla flavoring
1 cup chopped pecans

Combine everything but vanilla and pecans into skillet and cook until soft ball stage. (I cook to about 210° F instead of 238° F.) Set off heat and add vanilla. Cool until you can put your hand on the bottom of the skillet. Beat until gloss is gone. Put in pecans and pour in pans.

ZUCCHINI CRISP
Jimmie Russell

 Lodge 3 Qt. Deep Covered Skillet

6 cups zucchini, peeled and sliced like apples
3/4 cup sugar
3/4 cup water
1/4 cup Real Lemon bottled lemon juice
1 1/2 teaspoons cinnamon
1 1/2 tablespoons butter

Topping
1 stick butter
1 cup self-rising flour
1 cup quick oatmeal
3/4 cup brown sugar

Combine zucchini, sugar, water, lemon juice, and cinnamon in the deep skillet. Boil until zucchini is tender. Stir to keep from burning. Add butter and mix well. Preheat oven to 350° F. Mix topping ingredients until crumbly. Sprinkle on top of zucchini and bake for 30 minutes, until brown. Top with whipped cream or ice cream.

"As anyone who raises a garden knows, zucchini grows overnight! People here often joke about using them up before they multiply. This recipe which I prepare often for the Holly Avenue Methodist Church fellowship meals is a good way to use the zucchini. The members always think it is apple." - 2003

PEANUT BUTTER FUDGE
Patsy Sherrill

 Lodge 3 Qt. Deep Covered Skillet

3 cups sugar
3 tablespoons white Karo syrup
1 cup evaporated milk
1 stick butter or margarine
Dash salt
3 tablespoons peanut butter
1 teaspoon vanilla

Mix all ingredients together except for vanilla and stir until well blended in a deep iron pot, such as the deep skillet. Cook over medium heat, stirring often, until sugar dissolves. Increase the heat to medium-high and bring to a boil. Boil until it forms a soft ball, about 234° F on candy thermometer. Add vanilla and beat vigorously with electric mixer until gloss is gone. Pour into two buttered Pyrex dishes.

DIXIE PEANUT BRITTLE
Barbara Raulston Russell

 Lodge 3 Qt. Deep Covered Skillet

2 cups sugar
1 cup light corn syrup
1/2 cup water
1/2 teaspoon salt
2 tablespoons butter
3 cups raw peanuts (about 1 pound), skins on but shelled
2 teaspoons baking soda
Candy thermometer

In deep cast iron skillet, heat sugar, syrup, water, and salt and bring to a rolling boil. Add peanuts. Reduce heat to medium and stir constantly. Cook until syrup reaches 293° F on candy thermometer. Add butter, then baking soda. Remove from heat. Beat rapidly and pour on a buttered surface spreading to 1/4 inch thickness. When cool, break into pieces.

Mrs. Russell made this peanut brittle from peanuts they grew on their farm.

NEW ORLEANS PRALINES
Barbara Gonce Clepper

1 1/2 cups sugar
1 1/2 cups brown sugar
1 cup evaporated milk
1/4 cup butter
2 cups pecans, toasted
1 teaspoon pure vanilla
Candy thermometer

Bring sugars and milk to a boil in a deep iron pot. Cook over medium heat, stirring often, for 10 minutes or until candy thermometer registers 228° F. Stir in butter and pecans. Continue cooking, stirring constantly until candy thermometer registers 236° F. This is the soft ball stage. Remove from heat. Stir in vanilla. Beat with a wooden spoon for 2 minutes or until mixture begins to thicken. Quickly drop by heaping tablespoons onto buttered wax paper or slab of marble. Let candy stand until firm.

"When we lived in New Orleans in the early 70s, we always enjoyed watching the cooks making pralines in the candy shops."

Beverages

Whether you're enjoying a family gathering or simply relaxing on a lazy summer afternoon on the front porch, Southerners know how to keep cool with refreshing liquid libations. Usually sweet, never made with freeze-dried powdered mixes, and served among good friends...

GALA PUNCH

Phyllis Wilson

2 pounds sugar
16 cups water
2 large cans orange juice
3 large cans pineapple juice
3 bottles lemon juice
1 bottle almond extract
3 bottles ginger ale
1/2 gallon pineapple sherbet

Boil sugar and water for two minutes. Add juices and extract.
Chill. When ready to serve add ginger ale and sherbet.
Yield: 50 servings.

FRESH LEMONADE

Linda Cole

10 lemons
3 cups water
2 cups white sugar
4 cups crushed ice

Cut 1/2 of one lemon into thin slices and set aside. Juice
remaining 9 1/2 lemons and pour into a glass pitcher or punch
bowl. Stir in the water and sugar until dissolved. Pour in the
crushed ice and float the lemon slices on top.

SOUTHERN SWEET ICE TEA

3 family size tea bags
2 cups cold water
1 cup sugar

Place the two cups water in a pot and add the tea bags. Bring to a boil, do not continue boiling. Remove from heat and let steep for 20 -30 minutes. Pour warm tea into empty pitcher. Add the sugar and stir until the sugar is dissolved. Fill the pitcher the rest of the way full with cold water. Putting a wooden spoon into a glass pitcher before pouring in the hot liquid will prevent the glass pitcher from breaking.

SUN TEA

2 family size tea bags
1 quart water
Glass or translucent pitcher

Put the water and tea bags in the pitcher. Put in the sun and let sit. In about 30 minutes to an hour you have tea. Add cold water to desired strength. Refrigerate.

Index

Index By Ingredients